SEASONS OF WICCA

SEASONS OF WICCA

The Essential Guide to Rituals and Rites
to Enhance Your Spiritual Journey

AMBROSIA HAWTHORN

ILLUSTRATIONS BY
TRAVIS STEWART

**ROCKRIDGE
PRESS**

To my fellow Wiccans who are on a journey to enhance
their practice and deepen their faith.

Interior and Cover Designer: Emma Hall
Art Producer: Tom Hood
Editors: Natasha Yglesias and Crystal Nero
Production Manager: Michael Kay
Production Editor: Melissa Edeburn

Illustrations © Travis Stewart, 2020

ISBN: Print 978-1-64611-229-6 | eBook 978-1-64611-230-2

R0

CONTENTS

INTRODUCTION

Hello, and welcome to *Wiccan Rituals*, an essential guide to help new and experienced practitioners enhance their spiritual practice and deepen their faith. I'm Ambrosia, a Solitary Pagan and editor of *Witchology Magazine*, a monthly publication for modern witches. I'm both a Wiccan and witch who has dedicated 16 years to my eclectic practice. In this book, I'll be sharing my knowledge of Wicca, energy, magic, and rituals so you can enhance your own practice.

My journey into Wicca began after I stumbled upon magic at the age of 13. I began having dreams that often included a small door that led me into a world that looked exactly like my own yet was filled with enchanted magic. Usually, I would be walking in the woods, barefoot, behind my grandparents' house in Redwood Valley, California, and I would hear whispers from the wind and trees. These dreams and encounters left me feeling that there was something I needed to listen to or find. Not sure what I was searching for at the library and bookstores, I came across books about interpreting dreams. I spent hours combing through them, and eventually I found books on Wicca and witchcraft. As soon as I discovered these books, my heart began racing. This knowledge was what I had been seeking.

What began with those books blossomed into a lifelong journey of learning. Wicca became an integral part of my life, and though I now know the formalities, I still practice in a way that fits my own needs. Everyone has a different story or path, and your experiences and journey should shape your practice.

I hope this book will help you along your journey by providing valuable information to enhance your practice. Now, together, let's dive into the enchanting world of Wicca.

PART I
WICCA DEMYSTIFIED

Before we engage with the practice of Wicca, we need to discuss how it began and how it has evolved. I'll clarify Wicca's origins and beliefs so you can build your own successful, authentic Wiccan practice.

CHAPTER 1
WICCA'S ORIGINS & BELIEFS

In this chapter, I'll discuss the Wiccan Rede, the importance of working with nature and deities, the connection between magic and Wicca, and the ins and outs of building your own practice. These building blocks will enhance your spiritual practice and deepen your faith.

There are no governing bodies, recognized prophets, or true forms of Wicca. Many practitioners are drawn to Wicca because they're dissatisfied with the structure of traditional religions. Wicca attracts those who wish to embrace a path rooted in nature, spiritualism, and a reverence for the divine.

WHAT IS WICCA?

Wicca emerged in the United States in the 1960s as an Earth-centered religion that incorporates deity and ritual. Many believe the term *Wicca* originates from the English author Gerald Gardner, who is often referred to as the Father of Wicca. Gardner first used the term Wica, meaning "wise people," in his book *Witchcraft Today*, published in 1954. At the time, he referred to Wica as a tradition of witchcraft. Gerald Gardner's work was heavily influenced by others. As early as 1914, English occultist Aleister Crowley had the idea to create a new religion focused on nature and Pagan traditions. The origins of the rituals in Wicca can also be traced to scholar Margaret Murray, who in the 1920s wrote about witch cults and medieval religion. Murray is often referred to as the "Grandmother of Wicca."

Wicca falls under the umbrella term of *Paganism* and is sometimes associated with magic and witchcraft. Many practitioners use the terms *Wicca* and *witchcraft* interchangeably; however, not all Wiccans practice witchcraft, nor do all witches follow Wicca. Wicca's popularity as a modern religion is due in part to its inherent adaptability—it celebrates life and nature, and its practice is often unique to the individual.

THE WICCAN REDE

As you begin your exploration into Wicca, you will likely come across the Wiccan Rede. The Wiccan Rede is a statement that provides a guideline or moral compass for Wiccan practice, and it emphasizes the core value of doing no harm. (The term *rede* originates from the Old English *ræd*, which means "counsel" or "advice.")

There are multiple versions of the Rede, and its origins are cloudy. It was made famous in the 1960s by English Wiccan Doreen Valiente and in the 1970s by author Lady Gwen Thompson, who wrote a longer version titled *The Rede of the Wiccae*. Though there are multiple versions, the Redes all end with a form of the saying, *"Eight words the Wiccan Rede fulfill, An it harm none, do what ye will."*

NATURE

Engaging with nature is one of the primary tenets of Wicca, and many Wiccans are passionate about the environment and respect all forms of life. Nature permeates Wiccan practice by way of the elements, seasons, celebrations, tools, and even deities. Through the earth, Wiccans feel a connection to the divine, which is the basis for the sabbat, esbat, and solstice rituals.

Wiccan practice often uses tools from the earth, such as crystals, herbs, wooden items, feathers, bone, and minerals. There is energy in all these items. If you choose to practice magic, you can learn to harness that energy to manifest healing, protection, transformation, and prosperity. If you choose a magic- or witchcraft-free path, you might choose to celebrate Earth's changing seasons and to honor life, death, and rebirth. To connect with nature, you might wish to spend time outdoors, follow the planetary movements and cycles, and notice the natural rhythms in the world around you.

Many Wiccans celebrate and honor the five elements (earth, air, water, fire, and sprit), the four seasons (summer, autumn, winter, and spring), the solstices (winter and summer), the equinoxes (spring and autumn), the 13 full moons (esbats), Earth's position relative to the sun, and the eight Pagan sabbats (Samhain, Yule, Imbolc, Ostara, Beltane, Litha, Lughnasadh, and Mabon). I'll discuss all of these in greater depth throughout this book.

DEITIES

Goddesses and Gods play a vital role in Wicca. In some Wiccan traditions, the Gods and Goddess are all-encompassing deities and are sometimes referred to as the Horned God and Triple Goddess, God and Goddess, or Lord and Lady. These all-encompassing deities of Wicca are considered complementary polarities that represent the masculine and feminine essences of life. They are responsible for life and balance on Earth.

The Lord, God, Horned God, or masculine presence is represented by the sun, solstices, and fertility of the land and is often symbolized by animal horns, black candles, antlers, and phallic tools, such as swords and wands.

The Lady, Goddess, Triple Goddess, or feminine presence is represented in the cycles of the moon and the stages of womanhood, such as maiden, mother, and crone. The symbols that represent the feminine aspect are water, cups and vessels, and white candles.

Some traditions may honor or celebrate specific deities rather than all-encompassing deities. Choosing which specific deities to honor depends on the practitioner's beliefs and spiritual preferences. You can choose deities from any pantheon, but beginners often choose from the Celtic, Nordic, or Greek pantheons.

There are many ways to choose a deity to honor. One way is to seek corresponding themes. For example, if you're celebrating a sabbat, you might look for deities associated with that particular sabbat. Alternatively, if you want to hold a ritual to manifest prosperity or love, you might choose deities associated with those qualities.

MAGIC(K)

Wiccan magic, also referred to as *magic, magick, witchcraft, practical magic*, or *spellcasting*, is the manipulation and channeling of energy to harness power. By harnessing this power, you can influence the world around you to create positive change for yourself.

I mentioned earlier that some Wiccans don't practice witchcraft. It is possible to have a full Wiccan practice without harnessing energy or casting spells. If you chose this path, you'd be considered a Wiccan who lives in harmony with nature and who celebrates the changing seasons, sabbats, and deities without seeking to manipulate the energy found in nature. Of course, you can be a Wiccan who practices magic. Look within yourself and decide what feels right to you.

Those who intend to practice magic, or who are simply interested, must understand the terminology of "good magic" and "bad magic." These terms often show up on social media in both the magical and nonmagical communities. Magic is "gray" more than it is black and white, and it follows ethical rules. For instance, you wouldn't want anyone to perform a spell to harm, curse, or alter your own free will, so you shouldn't use magic to do that to others. Practicing magic comes with great responsibility, and it requires you to make ethical choices. Refer to the Wiccan Rede on page 4 whenever you practice magic.

To perform the rituals in this book, I recommend using magical tools to assist you. These tools are often used on your altar or in your magical workspace of choice. The tools will vary depending on your intentions, and they have significance and meaning that often reflect elements found in nature. The four most common elemental tools used in Wicca are the chalice, wand, athame, and pentacle.

The **chalice**, bowl, or cup represents the element of water, the Goddess or Lady, and often signifies feminine qualities. In the chalice, you'll often place water, wine, or other prepared mixtures.

The **wand** represents the element of air in most Wiccan practices and fire in most esoteric practices. A wand is used to help direct energy, assists with ritual circle creation, and symbolizes the God, Lord, or masculine presence. Often, wands are made of wood and sometimes incorporate clay and crystals.

The **athame** is a ceremonial blade that represents the element of fire, and like a wand, it also directs energy. Though athames are knives, they are not used for actual cutting; instead, they are used symbolically to "cut" through energy or to draw symbols in the air. Athames are often used interchangeably with wands.

The **pentacle** represents the element of earth. A pentacle is a circle containing a five-pointed, upright star and is often used or worn as a symbol of protection or of a witch's beliefs. In many of the rituals in this book, you'll place elemental items in a pentacle configuration, with items at each of the five points. The pentacle symbol is often inscribed or drawn on a round, flat object made of wood, metal, clay, or stone.

Other popular tools used to complement a Wiccan practice are candles, crystals, herbs and oils, incense, cauldrons, bells, besoms, bolines, offerings, ritual robes, a Book of Shadows, divination tools, songs and chants, and physical representations of deities and the elements. For further information on these items, see "Tools for Magical Transformations" (page 36).

COVENS & SOLITARY PRACTICE

Some Wiccans engage in a solitary practice, whereas others belong to covens, which is a group of practicing Wiccans. Neither type of practice is better than the other. New Wiccans usually begin as solitary practitioners, and once they get comfortable, they may seek out like-minded individuals to discuss with and learn from. This communication is one of the most popular reasons for joining a coven.

Some covens follow a more structured path or tradition, but that's not always the case. Although a coven can be a wonderful source of community for some, it's not ideal for everyone. Some instead join circles, which are popular, less-structured gatherings common in the magical community. Circles take place during a celebration such as a sabbat or esbat.

WHAT WICCA ISN'T

Distinguishing among Wicca, Paganism, and witchcraft can be a little difficult. If you're just beginning to explore these traditions, focus on looking within yourself and figuring out what feels right to you. Read as many books as you can, start practicing, and check in with yourself regularly to see what clicks. If you have an affinity for herbs, gardening, and healing, you may be drawn to a green or herbal path. If you're fascinated by dreams, astral travel, and meditation, explore those practices and see where they take you.

Common misconceptions about Wicca

Wicca is a cult. Wicca is an Earth-centered religion.

Wiccans worship the devil. Satan is an Abrahamic figure, not a Wiccan one.

Wiccans don't believe in God. Wicca is a polytheistic religion that honors the all-encompassing God and Goddess or multiple Gods and Goddesses from different pantheons or traditions.

Wicca has no rules. Wicca has no governing body, but it is guided by ethical practices and moral behavior.

CHAPTER 2
THE HEART
OF WICCA

In this chapter, we'll dive into the core concepts of Wicca, including the Wheel of the Year (and the eight *sabbats*) and the five elements. We'll discuss the four classical elements that make up the physical world (earth, fire, water, and air) and a fifth element often recognized in Wicca: spirit. Spirit, often referred to as *akasha* or *aether*, is the connection between the other elements and the bridge between the physical and spiritual worlds. These foundational concepts form the heart of Wicca, and they are vital to building and strengthening your practice.

RITUALS

Rituals are ceremonies or celebrations that are an integral part of Wiccan practice. They are often used to mark the sabbats, changing seasons, milestones, and esbats (full moons), or they are used to honor a deity. Rituals can help you grow spiritually and become closer to the God and Goddess.

Rituals differ from spells in a few ways. Spells are a set of steps for an intended purpose, such as healing, love, or prosperity. Rituals are generally more diverse and elaborate than spells, and they involve work with a deity for an intended purpose. Rituals sometimes include a spell.

Rituals are popular because they can be tailored to your practice. A formal ritual might include rigorous planning, self-cleansing and purification, an altar setup, casting of a protection circle, a meditation session, an offering to the deity, a rite or celebration, a giving of thanks and closing of the protection circle, and even cake and ale. A less formal ritual might consist of basic purification, casting a circle, a rite or celebration, and closing of the circle. I'll discuss ritual steps in greater detail in chapter 4.

The first decision to make before performing a ritual is to decide on the celebration or event you wish to honor, such as a full moon, a sabbat, or a major life event.

Next, it's important to purify both yourself and the area where you'll be performing the ritual. Purification refers to cleansing, consecrating, and charging (raising energy) in preparation for a ritual. Instructions for purification can be found on page 30.

After purification, it's time to prepare your altar for the ritual. An "altar" refers to a ritual workspace, which is where you place your magical tools and any physical representations of the ritual's theme or purpose. You can be creative when decorating your altar space, but remember to prioritize functionality and to work with what you have. Instructions for creating an altar can be found on page 31.

From there, you'll create or "cast" a circle of protection. When casting a circle, you use energy to create a sacred space or imaginary boundary surrounding your workspace. This energetic boundary separates your ritual from the everyday world and protects against outside forces or unwanted spirits. Instructions for casting and closing a circle can be found on page 33.

To finish the ritual, you can leave an offering for the deity or have a "cake and ale" ceremony in which you share an offering of food and drink with the deity to thank them for their blessing and time. More information about invoking and thanking a deity and cake and ale ceremonies can be found on page 35.

Above all, understand that there is no "best" path and no "correct" way to perform a ritual. The purpose of this book is to help practitioners of all paths enhance their spiritual practice through ritual. A Wiccan's journey shouldn't focus on being right or wrong, but, instead, focus on growing, learning, and accepting oneself and others through practice.

WHEEL OF THE YEAR

The Wheel of the Year comprises eight sabbats (or celebrations) that mark the changing seasons as Earth makes its journey around the sun. The eight sabbats include four solar festivals that mark the four seasons, also known as the *Lesser Sabbats*, and four Earth festivals that mark the midpoints between seasons. The Earth festivals are called the Greater Sabbats or cross-quarter days. The terms *greater* and *lesser* don't signify the relative importance of the sabbats; rather, they refer to the corresponding energies of Earth at the time. You can find rituals for the sabbats in chapter 5.

The solar festivals include the spring and autumn equinoxes, Ostara and Mabon, and the winter and summer solstices, Yule and Litha. The word *equinox* comes from the Latin word *aequinoctium*. *Aequi* means "equal," and *noct* refers to "night." As such, an equinox is a 24-hour period of equal night and day. The word *solstice* comes from two Latin words: *sol*, meaning "sun," and *sistere*, meaning "to stand still."

The two solstices are often represented by the Oak King and Holly King. The Oak King represents the waxing or growing sun during the light half of the year, and the Holly King represents the waning or dimming sun during the dark half of the year. Legend has it that during each solstice, the Oak King and Holly King battle. During Litha, the Holly King triumphs, and the Oak King triumphs during Yule.

The four Earth festivals—**Imbolc**, **Beltane**, **Lughnasadh**, and **Samhain**—mark the midpoints between the solar festivals. These sabbats are originally Pagan holidays, and they combine history, agriculture, culture, religion, folklore, and magic. Anglo-Saxons celebrated the solstices and equinoxes, whereas the Celts celebrated cross-quarter days, sometimes referred to as "fire festivals."

Along with these eight sabbats, Wiccans often celebrate esbats, or full moons. More information on esbats can be found in chapter 6.

Yule (*yool* or *ewe-elle*), also called Winter Solstice, Midwinter, Witch's Christmas, or Yuletide, is celebrated on December 21 to 22 in the Northern Hemisphere and June 21 to 22 in the Southern Hemisphere. It celebrates the longest night of the year and the rebirth of the sun, or victory of the Oak King. After Yule, the nights begin to shorten. Yule is a time to honor rebirth, transformation, the darkness of night, and the waning sun.

Imbolc (*im-bullg* or *im-bolk*), also called Candlemas, Imbolg, Brigid's Day, Lupercalia, or Oimelc, is celebrated on February 1 in the Northern Hemisphere and August 1 in the Southern Hemisphere. This is the first of the three spring festivals. It celebrates the time when life wakes up after winter. Imbolc is a time to honor fertility, love, and creativity.

Ostara (*oh-star-ah*), also called Spring Equinox, Vernal Equinox, or Eostra's Day, is celebrated on March 20 to 21 in the Northern Hemisphere and September 20 to 21 in the Southern Hemisphere. Ostara is the second of the three spring festivals. During this sabbat, the length of day and night is equal. Ostara is a time to celebrate renewal, balance, and rebirth.

Beltane (*bel-tyn* or *bel-al-tin-ah*), sometimes spelled Beltain and also called May Day, is celebrated on May 1 in the Northern Hemisphere and November 1 in the Southern Hemisphere. During this sabbat, the veil between life and death is thin (this also happens during Samhain). Many Wiccans use this time to work with spirits and fae (nature spirits such as fairies, elves, and goblins). Beltane is the third of the three spring festivals and is a time to celebrate new beginnings, passion, and romance.

Litha (*lie-tha* or *lee-tha*), also called Summer Solstice, Midsummer, or Midsummer's Eve, is celebrated on June 21 to 22 in the Northern Hemisphere and December 21 to 22 in the Southern Hemisphere. It celebrates the longest day of the year and the death of the sun, or victory of the Holly King. After Litha, the days grow shorter. Litha is a time to celebrate strength, the sun, vitality, and growth.

Lughnasadh (*loo-nah-sah*), also called Lammas or First Harvest, is celebrated on August 1 in the Northern Hemisphere and February 1 in the Southern Hemisphere. Lughnasadh is the first of the three harvest sabbats. It is a time to celebrate abundance, creativity, and gratitude.

Mabon (*may-bun*), also called Autumn or Fall Equinox, Harvest Home, and Witch's Thanksgiving, is celebrated on September 22 to 23 in the Northern Hemisphere and March 20 to 21 in the Southern Hemisphere. During this sabbat, the length of day and night is equal. Mabon is the second of the three harvest sabbats. It's a time to celebrate abundance and express gratitude.

Samhain (*sow-in* or *sah-win*), also called Hallowmas, Day of the Dead, All Hallows Eve, and Witch's New Year, is celebrated on October 31 in the Northern Hemisphere and April 30 in the Southern Hemisphere. Samhain is the third of the three harvest sabbats and a time when the veil between life and death is thin (as it is during Beltane). Many Wiccans use this time to honor their ancestors and deceased friends and pets, and to work with spirits. Samhain is a time to celebrate life, death, and endings.

FIVE ELEMENTS

The five elements—earth, air, water, fire, and spirit—are an integral part of Wicca. These elements are present in all life forms and make up the universe. Each cycle, deity, tool, moon, and event has an elemental correspondence and associations. Each element has a crucial purpose in providing guidance and energy in a Wiccan's practice. Many rituals invoke the elements for assistance, and you'll often place items on your altar to represent the elements. More information on elemental representations can be found on page 42.

EARTH

COLOR Green

CARDINAL DIRECTION North

PENTACLE PLACEMENT Lower left

STONES Emerald, onyx, jasper, salt, azurite, amethyst, quartz

GODDESSES Ceres, Demeter, Gaea, Mah, Nephtys, Persephone, Rhea

GODS Adonis, Athos, Arawn, Cernunnos, Dionysus, Mardyk, Pan, Tammuz

SEASON Winter

GENDER Feminine

ENERGY Receptive

QUALITIES Abundance, femininity, prosperity, grounding, stability, strength, wealth

ZODIAC SIGNS Capricorn, Taurus, Virgo

AIR

COLOR Yellow

CARDINAL DIRECTION East

PENTACLE PLACEMENT Upper left

STONES Topaz, pumice, rainbow stones, crystals, amethyst, alexandrite

GODDESSES Aradia, Arianrhod, Cardea, Nuit, Urania

GODS Enlil, Kheoheva, Merawrim, Shu, Thoth

SEASON Spring

GENDER Masculine

ENERGY Projective

QUALITIES The mind, communication, psychic powers, inspiration, imagination, ideas, knowledge, wishes

ZODIAC SIGNS Gemini, Libra, Aquarius

WATER

COLOR Blue

CARDINAL DIRECTION West

PENTACLE
PLACEMENT Upper right

STONES Aquamarine, amethyst,
blue tourmaline, pearl, coral,
blue topaz, fluorite

GODDESSES Aphrodite,
Isis, Marianne, Mari,
Tiamat, Yemaha

GODS Dylan, Ea, Manannan,
Osiris, Neptune, Poseidon

SEASON Autumn

GENDER Feminine

ENERGY Receptive

QUALITIES Emotion, absorption,
subconscious, purification,
eternal movement,
wisdom, soul

ZODIAC SIGNS Cancer,
Scorpio, Pisces

FIRE

COLOR Red

CARDINAL DIRECTION South

PENTACLE
PLACEMENT Lower right

STONES Ruby, fire opal,
volcanic lava, agate

GODDESSES Brigid, Hestia,
Pele, Vesta

GODS Agni, Horus,
Prometheus, Vulcan

SEASON Summer

GENDER Masculine

ENERGY Projective

QUALITIES Energy, inspiration,
love, passion, leadership

ZODIAC SIGNS Aries, Leo,
Sagittarius

SPIRIT

COLOR White

CARDINAL DIRECTION Central

PENTACLE PLACEMENT Top

STONES Any

DEITIES God and Goddess

SEASONS Entire Wheel
of the Year

GENDERS Universal

ENERGY Universal

QUALITIES Connection, presence,
balance, eternity

ZODIAC SIGNS Any

CHAPTER 3
POPULAR TRADITIONS

Since the 1950s, Wicca has continued to evolve from its original Gardnerian and Alexandrian traditions into newer traditions (Dianic, Celtic, and Solitary, for example) that are sometimes referred to as Neo-Wicca or modern Wicca. In this chapter, I'll explain the background of these particular Wiccan traditions to help you find a path that's right for you. More traditions are waiting for you to discover them.

THE GARDNERIAN TRADITION

The **Gardnerian** tradition, also called British Traditional Witchcraft, Gardnerian Wicca, or Gardnerian Witchcraft, refers to a group of individuals who follow the teachings of Gerald Gardner. The Gardnerian tradition, developed by Gerald Gardner in the United Kingdom in the 1950s, is often considered the earliest Wiccan tradition. At the time, however, Gardner referred to his teachings as witchcraft, not Wicca.

Gerald Gardner was born in Lancashire, England, in 1884 but spent many of his early years abroad, where he gained an appreciation for native cultures, rituals, and ceremonies. Gardner returned to England in the 1930s and began to study occultism and witchcraft. He was initiated into the New Forest coven, a group of witches who focused on beliefs and practices believed to predate Christianity. Much of the New Forest coven's work was inspired by Egyptologist Margaret Murray, who in the 1920s wrote about European witch cults. Gardner took his practices and experiences of ceremonial magic, his work from the New Forest coven, **Kabbalah**, and his occult findings and combined them to create a new tradition. The Gardnerian tradition worships two principal deities: the Horned God and the Mother Goddess.

Gardnerian tradition has three degrees that mark a Wiccan's journey of learning and practice. The **First Degree** is the initiation into the tradition, often in the form of a ritual and dedication ceremony. A year and a day after the First Degree, the practitioner can have a **Second Degree**. This degree represents advancement beyond the basics. After five to seven years of rigorous study and practice, one can achieve the **Third Degree**. The Third Degree often elevates a member to a leadership role in their coven or brings them one step closer to becoming a High Priest or Priestess. If and when the member becomes comfortable leading others, they may branch out and start their own coven.

Gardnerian tradition follows karmic law and focuses on not harming others. The practice is kept secret and bound by oath, so not many outside of Gardnerian tradition know the specifics of their practice. Gardnerian rituals are very elaborate and commonly involve ritual sex or nudity; in the tradition, nakedness is a sign of freedom and equality. Gardnerian tradition varies widely, with each coven having its own specificities and levels of observance, and is practiced all over the world.

THE ALEXANDRIAN TRADITION

The **Alexandrian** tradition, also called Alexandrian Wicca or Alexandrian Witchcraft, was founded in the United Kingdom and gets its name from its founder, Alex Sanders, and his wife, Maxine Sanders. The Alexandrian tradition has its origins in Gardnerian tradition; Alex Sanders was a member of a Gardnerian tradition before leaving it to start his own sect in the 1960s. Alexandrian tradition incorporates Gardnerian teachings with ceremonial magic and **Qabalah**.

Like the Gardnerian tradition, Alexandrian tradition also focuses heavily on ritual and ceremony and has degrees and initiation ceremonies, but it is not as secretive or strict with the rituals and rules. However, you will not find the Alexandrian tradition's Book of Shadows or rituals online; the only way to learn more about the practices of this tradition is to join it.

Alexandrian tradition is known for being eclectic, following a "use it if it works" philosophy and prioritizing the practitioner's growth. The tradition also emphasizes the polarities of masculine and feminine and honors the **Horned God** and the **Mother Goddess**. This tradition often involves ritual nudity (also called **skyclad**); however, practicing naked is optional in some covens. The Alexandrian tradition is practiced all over the world.

THE DIANIC TRADITION

The Dianic tradition is a feminist practice that focuses on the Goddess and often has women-only membership. This branch of Wicca uses the writings of author Zsuzsanna Budapest and originated in the United States during the 1970s.

The major difference between Dianic tradition and other traditions is that it honors only the Goddess deity, not the God. Dianic tradition emphasizes egalitarian matriarchy and gets its name from the Roman Goddess Diana. Members of the Dianic tradition will honor other Goddesses as well, but they treat them as parts of a single, monotheistic Goddess. The Dianic tradition focuses on the importance of womanhood and pulls from folk magic and various teachings of Gerald Gardner and Charles Leland, author of *Aradia, or the Gospel of the Witches*. Some Dianic covens reject transgender women, but there does exist a branch, founded by Morgan McFarland and her husband Mark Roberts, that accepts trans members.

THE CELTIC WICCA TRADITION

The Celtic Wicca tradition, like the Gardnerian tradition, follows two main deities—the Horned God and the Mother Goddess—but many practitioners of Celtic Wicca also follow other deities in the Celtic pantheon. One divine force celebrated in Celtic Wicca is the Triple Goddess, the female aspect often represented as Maiden, Mother, and Crone. This tradition combines the modern Wiccan tradition with Celtic mythology, history, and beliefs. Celtic Wiccans still use rituals and energy and celebrate nature, as do other Wiccan traditions.

Closely related to Celtic Wicca is Druidry, a spiritual path that embraces both the spiritual world and holistic medicine. Historically, Druids were priests, healers, poets, and philosophers, and much of Celtic Wicca incorporates elements of Druidism. Druidry and Wicca are two entirely separate paths, but they both honor Earth and the eight sabbats. Druidry is more focused on solar rituals, whereas Celtic Wicca often focuses on both solar and lunar rituals and deities. Wiccans who have an interest in the Celtic Wiccan tradition may find themselves looking into Druidry. Those who combine Wicca and Druid traditions sometimes call their practice Druidcraft.

THE SOLITARY WICCA

The Solitary tradition is a very popular way to practice the Wiccan craft. Solitary Wiccans practice Wicca alone, as an individual. Many who are new to Wicca start out as Solitary Wiccans while they develop their own path and study different traditions. Some later join traditions and others continue a solitary practice. Solitary Wiccans often adopt an eclectic path that is a collection of different traditions.

WHAT'S THE BEST WICCAN TRADITION FOR YOU?

The best tradition is the one that feels right to you, so when you're starting out, it's important to explore Wiccan traditions that you feel will meet your unique needs. If you have an interest in feminism, you might be drawn to Dianic Wicca, or if you have an interest in Celtic mythology and deities, Celtic Wicca may be more suited to you. Wherever your interests lie, the most important thing is to ask questions and learn as much as you can. If you're interested in learning more about a specific tradition, I recommend reading books about that tradition and reaching out to the magical community. Facebook groups, online forums, local meetups, and countless other sources of community can help you connect with Wiccans from different traditions or paths. Wicca is dynamic and always evolving, which means that as the tradition grows, new paths will continue to emerge. Finally, don't give up; if the first tradition you try doesn't feel right, keep looking and follow what feels good to you.

PART II
RITUALS TO ENHANCE YOUR SPIRITUAL JOURNEY

Before we dive into the specifics of the rituals, let's cover some basics that will take you one step closer to a rewarding spiritual journey. Bear in mind that evolving your spiritual journey is a lifelong process of give and take.

Everyone's spiritual journey is different, and what makes your journey unique is the fact that you have your own goals, ideas, and convictions. For some, spirituality is about devotion and faith; for others, it's about nurturing personal growth and fostering connections. Both of these—and nearly anything else—can be achieved through ritual.

When planning and preparing for your own rituals, it's important to remember that there is no "right" or "wrong" way. Just by practicing, you enhance your spiritual journey. Far more important than the outcome is the journey and what you learn along the way.

CHAPTER 4
RITUAL BASICS

Ritual basics provide a key foundation to a rewarding spiritual path. Without the basics, your rituals won't have meaning or intentions. In this section, I'll dive into the ritual basics of purification, setting up an altar, and casting a circle, and I'll teach you about the tools you can use for transformation. By starting out with the basics, you'll be equipped to perform the rituals contained in this book, and you might even be inspired to create your own. This chapter introduces many new terms, and for a quick reference, you can always consult the glossary on page 169.

ORDER OF RITUAL BASIC STEPS

1. Purification of self

2. Purification of space

3. Setting up your altar

4. Casting a circle of protection

5. Invoking a deity

6. Ritual observance

7. Thanking the deity

8. Cake and ale (optional)

9. Opening the circle

PURIFICATION

The first step in performing a ritual is the purification process of yourself and the space. Within this process are the three *C*'s: cleanse, consecrate, and charge. These concepts can be applied to your tools, your altar or room, and even to yourself.

Cleansing refers to cleaning yourself, your objects, and your space physically and spiritually. The easiest way to cleanse yourself is by taking a bath or shower to wash away any stagnant or unwanted energies. Next, you can put on a ritual robe or fresh clothing. To cleanse objects, you can pass them through the smoke of incense, water, or sweep them with a besom. To cleanse a room, use a smudge stick or besom to burn away or banish unwanted energy. Many of the rituals in this book instruct you to cleanse your altar. You can do this with a smudge stick, sweeping with a besom, sprinkling salt, or asperging water. More information on how to cleanse your altar in these ways can be found on page 45.

Consecration is the process of making a space or object sacred. To consecrate an object or space, you'll need to set your intentions and offer a blessing or call upon the elements to assist you. To call upon the elements, you can use physical representations for them on your altar, such as salt for earth, smoke for air, a candle for fire, or a bowl of liquid for water. Pass objects through the elemental representations and ask each element for its assistance in consecration.

Charging is the process of empowering, raising, or building energy for an intended purpose. You can raise energy to charge an item by singing, chanting, or meditating. You can also charge an object by leaving it out under a full moon to absorb the moon's energy. Crystals hold energy like batteries, so it's a great idea to charge your crystals during the full moon to have them ready for use in rituals at any time of the month. Be sure to cleanse and consecrate your crystals before you charge them.

SETTING UP YOUR ALTAR

An altar is your ritual workspace. It can be a table, an entire room, or an outdoor space—but it should be separate from where you sleep or spend time in everyday life. If you don't have a separate space, it will be necessary to set up, cleanse, consecrate, charge, and take down your altar each time you perform a ritual. Altars are meant to hold your magical tools and elemental and deity representations. Your altar is also a place to keep your Book of Shadows, cake and ale or other ritual offering, and any festive decorations.

Many Wiccans place their deity representation in the center of the altar and elemental representations in a layout according to their cardinal directions; others set up elemental representations according to their place in a pentacle configuration. The rituals in this book include instructions for either, but you can choose based on your preference. To set up elemental representations in a pentacle configuration, place spirit at the top, water at the upper right, fire at the lower right, earth at the bottom left, and air at the upper left. To set up elemental representations according to their cardinal directions, face the earth candle toward the north, the air candle toward the east, the fire candle toward the south, the water candle toward the west, and the spirit candle in the center.

Some Wiccans choose to work intuitively and create an entirely new altar arrangement depending on the ritual or event. For instance, if you're outdoors, you might place larger elemental representations in a circle around you. Take these suggestions and adapt them to fit your own practice.

CASTING A CIRCLE

Once you purify and set up your altar, you'll **cast a circle**. It's important to do this prior to beginning a ritual because casting a circle represents the space becoming sacred, thereby erecting a boundary around your space. Casting a circle will also protect you from unwanted attention or outside influences during your rituals.

You can use physical objects or visualize energy or light to create a boundary. Common physical boundary markers include salt, rope, candles, and crystals. You can also create a physical boundary with objects representing the elements. More information on tools to represent the elements can be found in the section "Tools for Magical Transformations" on page 36.

Casting a circle involves calling upon the **quarters**, cardinal directions, or elements to bless and protect your ritual space. To cast a circle, you will hold a wand or athame as an extension of your hand to assist with directing energy to create the boundary around the ritual space. Then, you'll call upon the elements.

First, turn to face the east and say something along the lines of: *"Element of air, I call on you; lend me your mental clarity."*

Next, you'll turn to the south and say: *"Element of fire, I call on you; lend me your power."*

Then, you'll turn to the west and say: *"Element of water, I call on you; lend me your fluidity."*

Finally, you'll return to the north and say: *"Element of earth, I call on you; lend me your stability."*

Once you have cast the physical elements, you can finish casting your circle with: *"With these physical elements, I cast a circle of protection."*

To include the fifth element, spirit, in your circle, you can replace the final statement with something along the lines of: *"With these elements, together with spirit, I cast a circle of protection above, below, within."*

A note: Some practices instruct you to begin casting a circle facing east, although others tell you to begin facing north. This is because some practitioners believe you should start with the element of earth, whereas others think you should end with earth. The decision is entirely up to the tradition you follow or your own intuition.

Once your circle is cast, you can move on to ritual observance.

When you have finished with the main part of your ritual, it's important to always open the circle to release the energy you called upon back to the elements. You'll release them in the opposite order that you called upon them.

Begin facing north. Say something like: *"Earth, I bid you farewell."*

Next, turn to the west: *"Water, I bid you farewell."*

Then, turn to the south: *"Fire, I bid you farewell."*

After that, turn to the east: *"Air, I bid you farewell."*

Finally, return to the north and open the circle by saying something like: *"Spirit, I bid you farewell. I open this circle and release the energy back into the earth."*

The general sequence stays the same, but what you say or invoke can be changed to fit your practice. Do you love to rhyme? Perhaps creating a couple of rhyming stanzas will work for you. Do you prefer chanting? If you do, creating a few lines to include repetition for chanting will be ideal. What's important is that you speak from the heart and are sincere when calling upon the elements or directions.

INVOKING AND THANKING A DEITY

After casting a circle of protection, you can invoke a deity for their assistance and blessings in your ritual. Many of the rituals in this book instruct you to have a representation or symbol of a deity on your altar so that you can call upon it. To represent a deity, you can use statues, visual references, or candles for the God and/or Goddess. More information on tools to represent deities can be found in the section "Tools for Magical Transformations" on page 36.

To invoke a deity, you can say something along the lines of: *"Lord and Lady, I invite you to join this circle tonight. Lend me your strength and grant your blessings."* If you want to invoke a specific deity, you can customize your invocation. For example, you could say: *"Brigid, Goddess of Fire and the Forge, I call and invite you here today."* Alter these invocations to fit your practice.

After you've called upon a deity, you can proceed with your ritual observance.

When you're finished, thank the deity for their assistance. Never dismiss a deity—only thank them. For example, to thank the Goddess Brigid for her presence, you can say something along the lines of: *"Brigid, Goddess of Fire and the Forge, I thank you for your presence here today. Accept my offering for lending me your strength and wisdom."*

Offerings are a popular way to show a deity appreciation for their support in your ritual. Examples of offerings include foraged items from nature, such as flowers and herbs that you can bundle together, handcrafted items, or a food and drink offering called **cake and ale**. More information on offerings and cake and ale can be found in "Tools for Magical Transformations" (page 36).

After the ritual, the offering left for the deity should be covered. The following day, any offerings that were cooked or foraged can be returned to the earth or burned. Any offerings that contain inorganic matter should be taken to a landfill or recycled appropriately.

TOOLS FOR MAGICAL TRANSFORMATIONS

I mentioned some basic tools for rituals on page 7—**chalice**, **wand**, **athame**, and **pentacle**—but there are many other methods to invoke magical manifestations. These include but are not limited to crystals, herbs, oils, candles, divination systems, a boline, bells, a besom, incense, a cauldron, songs, chants, and visual representations of a deity and elements. You can combine these tools or use them individually during rituals to support your intentions.

CANDLES are very popular in magical practice and are useful representations of elements and deities because they are easy to find and come in many colors, shapes, sizes, and materials (for example, beeswax, paraffin wax, gel, and plant waxes such as carnauba, palm, soybean, and bayberry). Tea lights have a burn time of 45 to 60 minutes, and votives have a burn time of three to four hours, though this may vary based on the material.

I recommend starting out with plain white tea light or votive candles because white candles can substitute for any other color. If you're ready to branch out, I recommend you get candles in colors to represent each of the elements (yellow for air, blue for water, green for earth, red for fire, and white for spirit) as well as a black candle. A black candle can represent the all-encompassing God, and a white candle can also represent the all-encompassing Goddess. The all-encompassing God is sometimes represented by a gold candle or a plain white candle with a God charm on it. As always, you can be as creative as you like when choosing your candles. As long as you set your intentions, you can adapt the colors to fit your preferences. When working with candles, always use fire-safe plates or candle holders.

INCENSE helps set the atmosphere during ritual practice. It can also represent the element of air. Incense assists with banishing negative energy, and when bundled into a smudge stick, it can be carried around a room to expel unwanted or stagnant energy. You can purchase premade incense or create your own. When working with incense, always use a fire-safe plate or incense holder.

CRYSTALS have a wide variety of uses and properties in magic. In rituals, they can be charged (see page 30) and used as a source of energy. They can also be used for healing, manifestation, and as representations of the elements. You can use crystals to mark a physical boundary when casting a circle (see page 33). Crystals can also be incorporated into athame handles, wands, and pentacles, or used for divination and crystal grids.

I recommend starting with clear quartz, which you can use as an all-purpose crystal. As you expand your crystal collection, you can use crystals in colors associated with the elements. Yellow stones (e.g., citrine, tiger's eye, and topaz) are associated with air, and their properties generally assist with the mind, communication, and logic. Blue stones (e.g., aquamarine, azurite, and lapis lazuli) are associated with water, and their properties generally assist with emotions, intuition, and healing. Green stones (e.g., peridot, agate, and jasper) are associated with earth, and their properties generally assist with wealth, success, and peace. Red stones (e.g., amber, carnelian, and garnet) are associated with fire, and their properties generally assist with vitality, energy, and passion. There is no designated physical representation for the element of spirit, but it can be represented by clear quartz crystals.

HERBS are some of the most popular tools in any magical practice. There exists an entire field of study dedicated to using herbs medicinally, but you don't need to be an expert to use herbs in your rituals; for instance, you can make a simple herbal tea. You can use the magical properties associated with different herbs to complement your rituals. For example, if you perform a ritual for creativity, you can incorporate the herb vervain into your ritual by sprinkling it over a candle or other object or brewing a tea with it for the cake and ale ceremony.

OILS are excellent mixed for a specific intention and can be used on your skin, to anoint magical tools, and to dress candles. Many rituals in this book ask you to use a combination of a carrier oil and essential oils. Carrier oils are skin-safe oils that can be used to dilute concentrated essential oils. Examples of popular carrier oils are olive, coconut, almond, jojoba, apricot kernel, and avocado. There are many essential oils, but the ones in this book are lavender, sage, lemon, orange, peppermint, frankincense, eucalyptus, and rosemary. You can purchase the oils or mix your own. To make your own mixtures, simply decide on a carrier oil, essential oil, and if you like, dried herbs.

These are just suggestions—you can get creative in using herbs and oils in your rituals. I recommend doing research online or getting a magical herbal reference book. The following books on herbs and oils are excellent resources:

Cunningham's Encyclopedia of Magical Herbs by Scott Cunningham

The Complete Book of Incense, Oils and Brews by Scott Cunningham

The Illustrated Herbiary: Guidance and Rituals from 36 Bewitching Botanicals by Maia Toll

 A CAULDRON is similar to a chalice or bowl and relates to the Goddess and femininity. Cauldrons are often made out of cast iron and can be used as a fire-safe bowl. Cauldrons are also used decoratively. Some practitioners keep two cauldrons, one for burning herbs or paper and another for mixing liquids and oils.

 A BELL is another popular altar tool to use during ritual to invoke a deity, banish negative energy, create harmony, and generate power through vibration. Bells are very versatile and can be used outside of rituals to banish unwanted spirits or energy throughout a home.

 A BESOM, or ritual broom, can sweep away old or stagnant energy before a ritual. A besom can also be used with a smudge stick or incense to help waft the smoke around a room. Besoms are ideal for quick cleansing before any magical work.

A BOLINE is a crescent-shaped blade that, unlike an athame, is used for physical cutting of herbs, ribbons, knots, and wood. Not many Wiccans use bolines, but cutting items come in handy for rituals, so some practitioners substitute bolines with other knives or scissors.

RITUAL ROBES are often worn to help separate the ritual from the everyday in a similar manner to a sacred space or altar that's created for any magical working. Members of covens often wear robes, and different colors can represent a practitioner's level or position. Ritual robes or clothing are often put on after a purification bath or shower.

ORACLE cards are a divination tool that can often be used directly out of the box, which makes them ideal for beginner readers. The Oracle system is less structured than other forms of divination such as Tarot or runes and can be used as you please; some practitioners build their own deck. Oracle decks can vary widely in style but usually come with 20 to 100 cards.

TAROT is a more advanced and structured divination tool of 78 cards divided into the major arcana (significant life events) and minor arcana (lesser, day-to-day life events). Tarot takes time and effort to learn, but if your intuition is strong, sometimes you can jump right in. One common misconception about Tarot is that you have to inherit or be gifted a deck. Some practitioners follow this rule, but it's not necessary. Learning about Tarot is about empowering yourself and listening to your own intuition. Find a deck that calls to you.

CASTING refers to tossing or throwing stones marked with symbols during divination. The most popular method of casting is rune casting. Runestones or runes are a set of stones marked with symbols of a Germanic alphabet called Futhark. Most runestones contain the 24-letter alphabet of the Elder or Older

Futhark. Each letter or rune symbol has a corresponding meaning that can be read during ritual to seek answers, receive messages, or gain insights. It's also popular to cast using Ogham staves, a set of wooden pieces marked with the symbols of the 20-letter Celtic alphabet that also correspond to different trees. Both of these methods of casting incorporate the element of earth, supporting a connection with nature.

 SCRYING is the practice of gazing into a surface to receive messages. Surfaces that can be used to scry are crystals, water, smoke, flame, or mirrors. A classic example of scrying is the age-old image of a fortune-teller gazing into a crystal ball. By focusing on a reflective surface, you can receive messages, visions, or images to interpret using your intuition. Scrying takes practice, but scrying during ritual is a great way to harness ritual energy.

SONG AND CHANTS are used in conjunction with a ritual to build up energy to support spells and rituals. There is power within words, so adding them to rituals or spells is popular. You can use words to invoke or call upon a deity or the elements. Songs and chants also come in the form of prayers and incantations. The words don't have to rhyme; how you structure or speak words in your ritual practice is up to you.

REPRESENTATIONS AND OFFERINGS

Many of the rituals in this book list tools such as elemental representations, deity representation, offering of choice, and cake and ale. Unlike many of the other specific tools used in rituals, these items give you an opportunity to be creative and use what feels right to you. Here, I'll provide some examples of items you can use in rituals that call for these more symbolic components.

ELEMENTAL REPRESENTATIONS

You have a great deal of choice when it comes to elemental representations for your altar. To represent the element of water, you can use a blue candle or water crystal, a bowl or chalice of water, a seashell, or pearls. To represent the element of earth, you can use a green candle or earth crystal, a bowl of salt, a pentacle, or a piece of wood. To represent fire, you can use any candle or crystal representing fire, lighter, or athame. To represent air, you can use a yellow candle or air crystal, incense, a besom, a feather, or a wand. Elemental triangle symbols (symbols that represent the elements) can also be inscribed on stones or candles. Some of the rituals in this book will ask you to use candles in elemental colors. This refers to candles in colors to represent the elements—yellow for air, blue for water, green for earth, red for fire, and white for spirit.

DEITY REPRESENTATIONS

Deity representations are physical representations of the God or Goddess you would like to invoke in your ritual. A deity can be represented by candles, statues, or images of the deity. Many practitioners have representations of the God and Goddess to invoke the masculine and feminine forces in nature during a ritual. Depending on your practice, you might decide to work with the God and Goddess or choose an individual deity. Many Wiccans start with a black (God) candle and a white (Goddess) candle and accumulate statues or other symbols over time.

OFFERINGS

Offerings, sacrifices, or traditional **cake and ale** are opportunities to exercise creativity in your practice. Frequently, offerings are foraged items, flowers, herbs, food and drink (cake and ale), or crafts made during the ritual. The term *cake and ale* refers to an offering of food and drink for the deity that is shared with anyone else partaking in the ritual. The "cake" is often a baked bread, biscuit, cookie, or cake, and the "ale" is a drink of your choosing. A cake and ale offering should be prepared ahead of time and portioned out to all participants, including the deity, during the process of thanking the deity. Many rituals in this book instruct you to leave an "offering of choice." Sometimes, the ritual includes suggestions for an offering, but if it doesn't, you can leave an offering of your preference.

FESTIVE DECORATIONS

Festive decorations are included in the instructions for many of the sabbat rituals in this book. Sabbats (sun celebrations) are more festive than esbats (moon celebrations) and other rites, so it's more common for festive decorations to be included in sabbats. Because sabbats are holidays that mark the changing of the seasons, the celebrations often include festive decorations that correspond to the season or month. Here are some common decorations for each sabbat.

YULE: holly, mistletoe, pine, wreaths, ornaments, Yule-specific decorations, or red, green, and white colors

IMBOLC: anything related to fire; red candles; Imbolc-specific decorations, such as a statue of the Goddess Brigid; Brigid's cross; and corn dolls

OSTARA: spring-themed decorations, such as flowers, eggs, and pastel colors

BELTANE: decorations related to fire or Beltane-specific decorations, such as the maypole, flower crowns, or fertility symbols

LITHA: decorations representing summer or the sun, orange or yellow items, or sunflowers

LUGHNASADH: harvest or August-related decorations, corn dolls, wheat, grain, corn, or autumn-hued items

MABON: decorations related to the harvest, autumn colors, root vegetables, apples, grapes, or even baskets

SAMHAIN: Halloween-inspired decorations, ancestor items, black and orange objects or candles, or items related to October

BOOK OF SHADOWS

A Book of Shadows is one of the most important components of every Wiccan's practice. The Book of Shadows is a unique record of rites, spells, rituals, meditations, recipes, and notes. Your Book of Shadows is what you make it—there is no right or wrong way to create or organize your magical journal. Many practitioners end up making one Book of Shadows for spells, one for rituals, and another for recipes. Some Wiccans even create volumes for different years. You can have many books or just one. It can be handbound, in a binder, or even digital. There are myriad options, and you can be as creative as you like. Doodles and pictures are helpful but not essential. If you need inspiration for decorating your Book of Shadows, you can search online for keywords relating to Book of Shadows to see what others have created and shared. It's important to note that your Book of Shadows is a record of your journey as a Wiccan or witch and therefore your book should be taken care of and cherished. Some Wiccans keep a Book of Shadows as well as journals. In such cases, the journals act as somewhere to jot down ideas. Once a ritual or spell is complete, it's carefully transferred to the Book of Shadows. This method is a great way to begin if you are concerned about messing up an expensive journal that you'd like to be your Book of Shadows. Who knows, maybe in the end you'll be happy with your messy journals just as they are. When creating your own Book of Shadows, have fun!

FREQUENT INSTRUCTIONS FOR RITUALS

Now it's time to dive into the heart of this book. You've learned how and why Wiccans cleanse and purify themselves and their spaces, and you've learned how to set up altars, cast circles, invoke a deity, and use various tools. You might have areas and items in your home that are already equipped and acceptable for ritual use. If so, all you'll need to do is purify them by performing the three C's (cleansing, consecrating, and charging) before use. Do you have to use every step and tool mentioned in this book? Absolutely not. Start simple, and after you have performed a few rituals, reflect and make any alterations accordingly. At the end of each ritual, clear the altar but leave the offering, if there is one.

Many of the rituals in this book include the same basic instructions. To familiarize yourself with them, here are some frequent references you'll come across.

1. Cleanse the altar/ritual area/space: Cleanse your surrounding area by smudging, sweeping, sprinkling salt, or asperging water.

   ➤ To purify with a smudge stick (a bundle of dried herbs bound with a string), light the smudge stick and pass it over the altar.

   ➤ To purify with a besom (a ritual broom), use the besom to sweep the altar.

   ➤ To purify with salt, sprinkle regular table salt over the altar (salt has associations with clearing, protection, and purification).

   ➤ To purify with asperging water, boil tap water to remove impurities or leave a bowl of water under a full moon to charge it and bless it with energy. This creates asperging water, which you can place in a bowl on, or sprinkle over, the altar.

2. Open the circle: Opening the circle is the process of releasing the called-on energy back to the elements, thereby returning the space to its pre-ritual state. Whenever you cast a circle and harness energy, you must reopen the circle to restore the balance of energy to equilibrium.

3. Release the elements: When casting a circle, you call upon each of the Guardians of the elements (or the elements themselves) to protect you for the duration of the ritual. Releasing the elements is the process of thanking and dismissing the Guardians of the elements one by one.

4. Reading Tarot, reading Oracle, casting rune stones, or reading Ogham staves: This is the process of using divination tools to interpret messages.

   ➤ To read Tarot or Oracle, shuffle the deck, fan it out, and pull one card for each question you would like to ask. Use the meaning of the Tarot or Oracle cards to interpret an answer.

   ➤ To cast rune stones (or runes), shake the bag of runes, focusing on your intentions, and pull out one rune for each question you have. Use the esoteric meaning of the rune to interpret an answer to your question.

   ➤ To read Ogham staves, shake the bag of staves and pull out one stave for each question you have. Use the esoteric meaning of the Ogham character to interpret an answer to your question.

You're almost ready to begin ritual practice, but I'd like to remind you of one last safety issue. When preparing for any ritual involving open flames, always keep a fire extinguisher ready or a fire safety system in place. Always work in a well-ventilated space and use fire-safe plates or candle holders to hold candles and incense sticks or cones. If using loose incense, burn it on a charcoal disc on top of a fire-safe plate. Never leave flames unattended, and do not allow fire near any fabric, curtains, or blinds. In the unlikely event that fire or smoke starts to get out of control, always prioritize your own safety.

CHAPTER 5

SUN CELEBRATIONS (SABBATS)

As previously discussed, many Wiccans celebrate the major solar movements known as the **solstices**, **equinoxes**, and the **midpoints** or **cross-quarter days**. These dates divide the year up into eight sabbats. They are **Yule** (the **Winter Solstice**), **Imbolc**, **Ostara** (the **Spring Equinox**), **Beltane**, **Litha** (the **Summer Solstice**), **Lughnasadh**, **Mabon** (the **Autumn Equinox**), and **Samhain**.

Each year, the orbit of Earth around the sun repeats and is celebrated through these eight sabbats. This chapter includes two rituals for each sabbat, connecting you to the power of the sun's movements. These rituals are designed mostly for solitary Wiccans, but each ritual can be adapted to fit the needs of a group or coven. To alter the ritual, divide the steps among the members of the group. Last but not least, remember to practice fire safety!

WINTER SOLSTICE

The Winter Solstice, also known as midwinter or Yule, marks the longest night of the year and is dedicated to the rebirth of the sun. Prior to the Winter Solstice, Earth is slumbering, waiting for the sun's strength to return. The rituals in this section are ideal for midwinter reflections and Yuletide festive blessings.

MIDWINTER REFLECTION RITUAL

Midwinter is the ideal time to perform a ritual for reflection. As Earth slumbers, waiting to reawaken, we humans also go through a dormant phase, waiting to move forward along with the sun's return. With this ritual, you can reflect on the deeper meaning of the changes occurring during this part of the year.

Ritual Setting
Altar

Tools and Supplies

Festive decorations for Yule— evergreens, pinecones, poinsettias, red and green colors

Deity representation—statues or images of the God and Goddess or a Yule deity

5 tea light or votive candles— elemental colors

Fire-safe plates or candle holder and incense holder

1 cone or stick incense—peppermint, frankincense, pine, myrrh, bayberry, or cinnamon

Lighter or matches

12 crystals or stones on hand or foraged from nature (to represent the months of the year)

Wand or athame

Tarot deck, runestones, or other divination system

Journal and pen

Offering of choice—bread, baked goods, crafted items, or foraged flowers and herbs

PRIOR TO THE RITUAL

1. Shower or bathe, visualizing all old or unwanted energies leaving your being.

2. Cleanse the altar.

PREPARING THE ALTAR

Place the festive decorations, deity representation, and tools on the altar. Place the elemental candles on fire-safe plates facing their respective cardinal directions. Light the incense on a fire-safe plate at the top of the altar, above the earth candle. Place the 12 crystals or stones in a pile to the left of the candles.

THE RITUAL

1. Cast a circle of protection. Hold the wand or athame as an extension of your hand to gather and direct energy as you call upon the elements. Starting from the east and ending north, call upon the element of air for mental clarity, the element of fire for power, the element of water for fluidity, and the element of earth for stability.

2. Invoke your chosen deities by saying: *"Lord and Lady, I invite you to join this circle tonight. Lend me your strength and grant your blessings."*

3. Light the incense. Close your eyes and spend 5 to 10 minutes reflecting on your year thus far. Allow the incense to guide and relax your mind as you think about the year's highs and lows.

4. Light the candles, saying: *"Candles of the elements, share with me your warmth and guiding light."*

5. Take a crystal or stone in your left hand. Set your intention for it to represent the month of January. Holding it in your left hand, pass it over all the candles until your hand is above the spirit candle. Transfer the stone into your right hand, pass it right across the altar, and place it to the right of the candles. This represents your journey in January and all that you have learned. If needed, spend extra time reflecting on this month.

CONTINUED

6. Repeat step 5 with each crystal or stone until all 12 are to the right of the candles.

7. Shuffle the Tarot deck or shake the runestones. Draw 12 cards or stones, one for each month of the year ahead.

8. Study the cards or stones and write down the results in the journal to reflect on later.

9. Thank the deities for their presence by saying: *"Lord and Lady, I thank you for your presence and assistance tonight. Accept my offering I created for you, and go if you desire or stay if you'd like."*

10. Release the elements in reverse order by beginning facing the north and ending east, thanking each element for their assistance and bidding them farewell. Then open the circle by saying: *"I open this circle and release the energy back into the earth."*

11. Extinguish the candles and incense or allow them to burn out. Leave the offering on the altar.

FESTIVE YULETIDE BLESSING RITUAL

A festive blessing ritual is ideal to celebrate Yule or for a holiday party or feast. Ideally, the ritual should be held in an area of your home where you enjoy company. This ritual can be done with your loved ones or as a solitary act before a feast.

Ritual Setting

Dining room table or area where food can be served

Tools and Supplies

Festive decorations for Yule

Wand or athame

Elemental representations

Deity representation

3 taper or votive candles—white, red, and green

Fire-safe plates or candle holders

Lighter or matches

Bell

Chalices or cups (one for each person partaking in the blessing)

Plate of food from feast (as offering)

Drink of choice

PRIOR TO THE RITUAL

1. Shower or bathe, visualizing all old or unwanted energies leaving your being.

2. Cleanse the altar.

PREPARING THE ALTAR

Place the festive decorations and tools on the dining room table. The table will act as the altar. Prepare the food and drink for the festivities. Place the candles on fire-safe plates on the table. Place the deity representation in an area that feels right to you. Place the elemental representations around the room in a pentacle configuration or facing the cardinal directions (see page 31).

CONTINUED

THE RITUAL

1. Cast a circle of protection. Hold the wand or athame as an extension of your hand to gather and direct energy as you call upon the elements. Starting from the east and ending north, call upon the element of air for mental clarity, the element of fire for power, the element of water for fluidity, and the element of earth for stability.

2. Invoke your chosen deities by saying: *"I welcome the Lord and Lady. Watch over this feast tonight, grant us Yuletide blessings, and accept the offering I gift to you."*

3. Light the candles and ring the bell to shift the energy in the room and commence the celebration feast.

4. At the end of the celebration, leave a plate of food as an offering to thank the Lord and Lady, and say: *"I thank you for your presence this merry night."*

5. Release the elements in reverse order by beginning facing the north and ending east, thanking each element for their assistance and bidding them farewell. Then open the circle by saying: *"I open this circle and release the energy back into the earth."*

6. Extinguish the candles and cover the food offering. Dispose of the offering the next day.

IMBOLC

Imbolc is the first of the three spring festivals and takes place directly between the Winter Solstice and the Spring Equinox. The rituals in this section support love and creativity.

IMBOLC RITUAL FOR LOVE

This ritual for love can be used to attract love into your life or to manifest self-love. Perform this ritual on Imbolc or during the month of February, when love is in the air thanks to Valentine's Day. This simple ritual uses fire, your desires, and rose petals.

Ritual Setting
Altar or outdoors

Tools and Supplies

Festive decorations for Imbolc—hearts, red cloth, rose quartz stones, or fresh flowers

Wand or athame

Elemental representations

Deity representation

Pen and paper

Fire-safe cauldron, if indoors, or firepit, if outdoors

Lighter or matches

4 or 5 dried rose petals

PRIOR TO RITUAL

1. Shower or bathe, visualizing all old or unwanted energies leaving your being.

2. Cleanse the altar.

PREPARING THE ALTAR

Place the festive decorations and tools on the altar. Place the elemental representations in a pentacle configuration or facing their respective cardinal directions around your fire area. Place the deity representation at the top of the altar.

CONTINUED

THE RITUAL

1. Cast a circle of protection. Hold the wand or athame as an extension of your hand to gather and direct energy as you call upon the elements. Starting from the east and ending north, call upon the element of air for mental clarity, the element of fire for power, the element of water for fluidity, and the element of earth for stability.

2. Invoke the Lord and Lady or love deity by saying: *"Lord and Lady (or name of love deity), I invite you to join this circle tonight. Lend me your strength and grant your blessings."*

3. Using the pen and paper, write down the things that you want to attract and manifest in your life. Be as specific as you can.

4. Fold the paper and put it in the fire-safe cauldron or firepit.

5. If not using a lighter, ignite a match and toss it on top of the paper.

6. Sprinkle the rose petals over the flames and say: *"Burning blaze, hear my desire, accept these petals and my request to manifest love from this fire."*

7. When you are ready, thank your chosen deity: *"Lord and Lady (or name of love deity), I thank you for the strength you share and the blessings you give."*

8. Release the elements in reverse order by beginning facing the north and ending east, thanking each element for their assistance and bidding them farewell. Then open the circle by saying: *"I open this circle and release the energy back into the earth."*

9. Sprinkle any leftover ash into the wind as an offering.

BRIGID CREATIVITY RITUAL

Imbolc has associations with fire, creativity, and the Goddess Brigid, who is associated with crafts of any kind, so connecting with her is ideal for sparking creativity. This ritual uses a connection to a specific Celtic Goddess, an orange candle to represent creativity, and an oil.

Ritual Setting
Altar

Tools and Supplies

Festive decorations for Imbolc— orange cloth, fresh flowers, Brigid's cross, or Imbolc items

Wand or athame

Elemental representations

Deity representation for Brigid

1 pillar or taper candle—orange

Fire-safe plate or candle holder

Oil, for anointing—olive, sweet almond, or apricot kernel

Lighter or matches

Cake and ale—homemade treats and a drink of your choice

PRIOR TO THE RITUAL

1. Shower or bathe, visualizing all old or unwanted energies leaving your being.

2. Prepare the cake and ale.

3. Cleanse the altar.

PREPARING THE ALTAR

Place the festive decorations and tools on the altar. Place the candle on the fire-safe plate. Place the elemental representations in a pentacle configuration around the candle or facing their respective cardinal directions. Place the deity representation at the top of the altar.

CONTINUED

THE RITUAL

1. Cast a circle of protection. Hold the wand or athame as an extension of your hand to gather and direct energy as you call upon the elements. Starting from the east and ending north, call upon the element of air for mental clarity, the element of fire for power, the element of water for fluidity, and the element of earth for stability.

2. Invoke the Goddess Brigid by saying: *"Brigid, Goddess of Fire and the Forge, I call and invite you here today."*

3. Anoint the candle with the oil to increase the potency of its energy. To anoint the candle, pour oil near the top of the candle and use your hands to rub the oil down the candle. Be careful not to get oil on the wick.

4. Light the candle and say: *"Great Goddess, bestow upon me your power and guidance and lend me your power of creativity."*

5. Spend 10 to 20 minutes in meditation, focusing on your intentions and on Brigid. Feel her fiery energy wrap around you and let yourself fall into a centered state.

6. When you feel ready, thank Brigid by saying: *"Brigid, Goddess of Fire and the Forge, I thank you for your presence here today. Accept my offering for lending me your strength and wisdom."*

7. Set out a portion of the cake and ale offering for Brigid. Then take a bite and have a sip of your own.

8. Release the elements in reverse order by beginning facing the north and ending east, thanking each element for their assistance and bidding them farewell. Then open the circle by saying: *"I open this circle and release the energy back into the earth."*

9. Extinguish the candle. Cover the cake and ale offering and leave it on the altar overnight. The next day, dispose of it by returning it to the earth.

OSTARA

Ostara, also known as the Spring Equinox, is a time of renewal, balance, and rebirth. It's the second spring festival of the year and is associated with the fertility of the land. The rituals in this section focus on honoring balance and celebrating renewal.

WEAVING BALANCE RITUAL

Honoring balance during Ostara is a perfect way to celebrate the equal daytime and nighttime of the Spring Equinox. In this ritual, you'll use string or yarn to create a woven representation of harmony.

Ritual Setting
Altar

Tools and Supplies

Festive decorations for Ostara—crystals, flowers or candles

Wand or athame

Elemental representations

Deity representation

1 cone or stick incense—lavender, rose, violet, or frankincense

Fire-safe plate or incense holder

Lighter or matches

3 (18-inch) pieces of string or yarn

6 miniature bells with loops (to hang on string)

PRIOR TO THE RITUAL

1. Shower or bathe, visualizing all old or unwanted energies leaving your being.

2. Cleanse the altar.

PREPARING YOUR ALTAR

Place the festive decorations and tools on the altar. Place the elemental representations facing their respective cardinal directions. Place the deity representation at the top of the altar. Place the incense on the fire-safe plate.

CONTINUED

THE RITUAL

1. Cast a circle of protection. Hold the wand or athame as an extension of your hand to gather and direct energy as you call upon the elements. Starting from the east and ending north, call upon the element of air for mental clarity, the element of fire for power, the element of water for fluidity, and the element of earth for stability.

2. Light the incense and meditate for 5 to 10 minutes on what it means to honor balance for yourself.

3. Hold the three pieces of yarn or string together and tie them in a knot at one end. Lay the knotted string on a flat surface so it is easy to braid. If you'd like, tape down the knot to keep it in place.

4. Hold the leftmost string, cross it over the middle string so it becomes the new middle string, and say: *"Goddess of the Moon and Night, I invite you to join me today."*

5. Hold the rightmost string, cross it over the current middle string so it becomes the new middle string, and say: *"God of the Sun and Day, I invite you to join me today."*

6. Take the new leftmost string, cross it over the current middle string so it becomes the new middle string, and say: *"I now join with the God and Goddess on this day of balance."*

7. Continue weaving the braid. As you braid, string on the bell charms. Once the braid is finished, lay it on the altar and say: *"With each strand, I honor the balance of life found in the changing seasons, celebrating equal night and day as the sun crosses the celestial equator, growing in strength. With this braid, I pay tribute to life's endings and new beginnings as Earth further awakens from its slumber. I thank the God and Goddess for their support and presence here today."*

8. Release the elements in reverse order by beginning facing the north and ending east, thanking each element for their assistance and bidding them farewell. Then open the circle by saying: *"I open this circle and release the energy back into the earth."*

9. Allow the incense to burn out. Leave the braid on the altar as an offering.

SPRING RENEWAL RITUAL

On Ostara, nature is resurrected after the harshness of winter. In this ritual, you'll work with the season of life and growth, using cardboard egg cartons to start a spring seedling garden that celebrates renewal. After the seedlings have grown, the egg carton can be cut apart for individual planting of the seedlings.

Ritual Setting

Outdoor altar (or any area that you can get dirty with soil)

Tools and Supplies

FOR THE RITUAL

Wand or athame

Elemental representations

Deity representation

FOR THE SEEDLINGS

Cardboard egg carton with 6 or 12 cells

Scissors

Waterproof tray or plate

Potting soil

Seeds of choice

Spray bottle with water

PRIOR TO THE RITUAL

1. Shower or bathe, visualizing all old or unwanted energies leaving your being.

2. Choose an outdoor altar or other workspace that can get a little dirty.

3. Cleanse the area.

4. Prepare the egg carton to hold seedings. To do this, cut the lid off an egg carton with the scissors. Poke a small hole in the bottom of each egg cell to support drainage. Place the egg carton on a waterproof drainage tray.

PREPARING THE ALTAR

Place the tools and supplies on the altar. Place the elemental representations in a pentacle configuration around the workspace. Leave room in the center for the egg carton. Place the deity representation at the top of the altar.

THE RITUAL

1. Cast a circle of protection. Hold the wand or athame as an extension of your hand to gather and direct energy as you call upon the elements. Starting from the east and ending north, call upon the element of air for mental clarity, the element of fire for power, the element of water for fluidity, and the element of earth for stability.

2. Invoke the God, Goddess, or other deity of your choice by saying: *"Deity, I invite you to join this sacred circle."*

3. Fill each egg cell with soil. Then, sprinkle 3 or 4 seeds into each cell. As you do this, say: *"Slumbering Earth, awaken. Allow these seeds to spring forth."*

4. Cover the seeds with a thin layer of potting soil and say: *"Lord and Lady, bless these seeds to grow with life renewed."*

5. Use the spray bottle to mist the seeds lightly with water. Meditate for 5 to 10 minutes on life and renewal.

6. Thank your chosen deity by saying: *"Deity, I thank you for the wisdom you share and the blessings you give."*

7. Release the elements in reverse order by beginning facing the north and ending east, thanking each element for their assistance and bidding them farewell. Then open the circle by saying: *"I open this circle and release the energy back into the earth."*

8. Place the seedlings where they will get the correct amount of sun. For this information, follow the instructions on the seed packets.

9. Water the seeds according to the packet instructions and watch them grow. What you grow will serve as an offering to the Lord and Lady.

BELTANE

Beltane, the third spring festival, is a time when the sun begins to overtake the night as the Summer Solstice approaches. During Beltane, the land is fertile and life is abundant, so it's the perfect time to celebrate growth and new beginnings.

MEDITATION GROWTH RITUAL

The growth we observe during the time surrounding Beltane makes the festival an ideal time to celebrate your own growth in life. This ritual will allow you to pause and focus on yourself. You'll make use of foraging, meditation, and the outdoors to ground and connect yourself with nature.

Ritual Setting
Outdoors

Tools and Supplies
1 piece foraged wood, to use as a wand

7 foraged stones—5 to represent the elements and 2 to represent deities

PRIOR TO THE RITUAL

1. Shower or bathe, visualizing all old or unwanted energies leaving your being.

2. Go outdoors and forage for stones and wood. Notice which colors, shapes, sizes, markings, or other attributes of each item call out to you.

3. Find an area outside where you will be comfortable sitting. A shady spot under a tree would be wonderful.

4. Mentally cleanse and set your intentions for each foraged item.

PREPARING THE WORSHIP AREA

Mentally cleanse the area by pushing your own energy into the space. Use the elemental and deity stones to create a circle around you.

THE RITUAL

1. Sit in the middle of the circle.

2. Cast a circle of protection. Hold the piece of foraged wood as an extension of your hand to gather and direct energy as you call upon the elements. Starting from the east and ending north, call upon the element of air for mental clarity, the element of fire for power, the element of water for fluidity, and the element of earth for stability.

3. Invoke the God, Goddess, or other deity of your choice by saying: *"Deity, I invite you to join this sacred circle."*

4. Close your eyes and sit in a comfortable position. Allow yourself to feel and listen to the world around you. Feel the earth beneath you. Listen to the breeze winding through the trees. If you're under the sun, can you feel its warming rays?

5. Focus on your intentions for growth and allow any messages or thoughts to flow freely. Once you feel in sync with the earth, meditate for 20 minutes.

6. When you have finished meditating, thank your chosen deity by saying: *"Deity, I thank you for the wisdom you share and the blessings you give."*

7. Release the elements in reverse order by beginning facing the north and ending east, thanking each element for their assistance and bidding them farewell. Then open the circle by saying: *"I open this circle and release the energy back into the earth."*

8. Use your foraged items to create a geometric shape or pattern as an offering to deity. Allow yourself to feel lighter as you return to your normal daily routine, leaving hindrances behind and letting yourself grow.

BELTANE FLOWER RITUAL

This ritual invokes the May Queen and King, two deities that represent flowers, the forest, nature, life, and other elements of spring. Here, the May Queen and King will lend their energy as you create a floral crown to embody the season when many flowers are in bloom. Beltane is the perfect time to honor nature's abundant life. Wear this crown when dancing or at an event, or save it as a decoration.

Ritual Setting
Altar

Tools and Supplies

FOR THE RITUAL

Wand or athame

Elemental representations

Deity representation—statues of May Queen and King, or candles

Lighter or matches

1 cone or stick incense—patchouli, mugwort, orange, rose, or frankincense

Fire-safe incense plate

FOR THE CROWN

Floral wire

Wire cutters

Floral tape

Fresh flowers and greenery—foraged, picked, or purchased

Spool of twine or ribbon

Boline or scissors

PRIOR TO RITUAL

1. Shower or bathe, visualizing all old or unwanted energies leaving your being.

2. Cleanse the altar.

PREPARING THE ALTAR

Place the tools and crown-making supplies on the altar. Place the elemental representations in a pentacle configuration. Place the representations of the May Queen and King deity at the top of the altar.

THE RITUAL

1. Cast a circle of protection. Hold the wand or athame as an extension of your hand to gather and direct energy as you call upon the elements. Starting from the east and ending north, call upon the element of air for mental clarity, the element of fire for power, the element of water for fluidity, and the element of earth for stability.

2. Light the incense on the fire-safe plate and invoke the May Queen and King: *"May Queen, Goddess of the Flowers and Spring's Breeze, May King, God of the Forest and Gusting Winds, join me today to honor nature and its abundant life."*

3. Trim and shape the floral wire to the desired size and fit so that it will sit loosely on your head. Twist the ends to create a circle and cover them with floral tape.

4. Add a layer of greenery around the wire, securing the pieces with floral tape.

5. Add a second layer of flowers over the greenery, securing the pieces with floral tape.

6. Once your crown is finished, create a bundle of leftover flowers and greenery to leave as an offering to the May Queen and King. When you are finished, say: *"By the powers of nature, I combine these flowers and honor Beltane. I thank the May Queen and King for your presence here today; you may go if you desire. Your presence will be forever felt through this crown of flowers."*

7. Release the elements in reverse order by beginning facing the north and ending east, thanking each element for their assistance and bidding them farewell. Then open the circle by saying: *"I open this circle and release the energy back into the earth."*

8. Extinguish the incense or allow it to burn out. Leave the flower crown on the altar as an offering.

LITHA

Litha, the Summer Solstice, is the longest day in the Wheel of the Year—a day when the sun is at its full strength. The rituals in this section focus on the energy and strength of the sun.

DRAWING DOWN THE SUN RITUAL

In this ritual, you'll pull in the power of the sun and draw its energy into a crystal. The crystal can then be used to charge your own spiritual battery during the darker months to come. There's no better time to perform this ritual than during the Summer Solstice, when the sun is at its strongest.

Ritual Setting
Outdoors, under the sun

Tools and Supplies

Festive decorations for Litha—flowers, seasonal altar cloth

Wand or athame

Elemental representations

Deity representation

1 pillar candle—orange, yellow, or red

Fire-safe plate or candle holder

Lighter or matches

1 crystal—citrine or quartz

Cake and ale—sun-shaped cookies or orange-flavored treats and cider, wine, or juice

PRIOR TO THE RITUAL

1. Shower or bathe, visualizing all old or unwanted energies leaving your being.

2. Prepare the cake and ale offering.

3. Find an area outdoors to set as the altar and cleanse it.

PREPARING THE ALTAR

Place the festive decorations and tools on the outdoor altar. Place the elemental representations in a pentacle configuration around the area. Place the deity representation at the front of the space. Place the candle on a fire-safe plate in the center of the elemental representations.

THE RITUAL

1. Cast a circle of protection. Hold the wand or athame as an extension of your hand to gather and direct energy as you call upon the elements. Starting from the east and ending north, call upon the element of air for mental clarity, the element of fire for power, the element of water for fluidity, and the element of earth for stability.

2. Invoke your chosen deities by saying something like: *"Great Goddess, I greet you! Share your love and light. Great God, I greet you! Share your strength and energy."*

3. Light the candle. Feel its strength and the warmth of the sun's energy.

4. Hold the crystal in your hand. Pass it through the warmth of the flame and say: *"With this crystal, I store the energy of the sun to carry with me during the darker months ahead."*

5. Portion out a cake and ale offering for the God and Goddess and say: *"Blessed Goddess, blessed God, I thank you for your presence in my circle here today and in my life always."*

6. Before ending the ritual, take a bite and have a sip of your cake and ale.

7. Release the elements in reverse order by beginning facing the north and ending east, thanking each element for their assistance and bidding them farewell. Then open the circle by saying: *"I open this circle and release the energy back into the earth."*

8. Extinguish the candle or allow it to burn out. Cover the cake and ale and leave it on the altar overnight as an offering. The next day, dispose of it by returning it to the earth.

9. Use your infused crystal when you need the strength of the sun in your life.

MIDSUMMER HEALING RITUAL

There's more to the sun than its strength and energy. You can make use of the midsummer sun to help yourself heal from past heartache, trauma, or depression. This spell uses fire to burn away and banish unwanted feelings and pain.

Ritual Setting
Altar

Tools and Supplies

Festive decorations for Litha—flowers, seasonal altar cloth

Wand or athame

Elemental representations

Deity representation

Pen and paper

Lighter or matches

Fire-safe cauldron

1 ounce dried parsley or basil

Runestones or Ogham staves

PRIOR TO THE RITUAL

1. Shower or bathe, visualizing all old or unwanted energies leaving your being.

2. Cleanse the altar.

PREPARING THE ALTAR

Place the festive decorations and tools on the altar. Place the elemental representations in a pentacle configuration. Place the deity representation at the top of the altar.

THE RITUAL

1. Cast a circle of protection. Hold the wand or athame as an extension of your hand to gather and direct energy as you call upon the elements. Starting from the east and ending north, call upon the element of air for mental clarity, the element of fire for power, the element of water for fluidity, and the element of earth for stability.

2. Invoke your chosen deities by saying something like: *"Deities of the Summer Solstice, I invite you to my sacred circle."*

3. Using the pen and paper, write down your negative feelings and anything else you want to banish from yourself.

4. Fold the paper, and begin burning a corner of the note. Once the paper is burning, place the note in the fire-safe cauldron.

5. While the note burns, sprinkle the parsley onto the flames and say: *"Burning flame, erase my pain and banish my hurt; healing herb, soothe my heart and mend my mind."*

6. While the note and herbs burn out, cast the runestones or read the Ogham staves, asking how you can further facilitate healing.

7. Thank the deities for their presence by saying: *"Deities of the Summer Solstice, I thank you for your strength and blessings."*

8. Release the elements in reverse order by beginning facing the north and ending east, thanking each element for their assistance and bidding them farewell. Then open the circle by saying: *"I open this circle and release the energy back into the earth."*

9. Allow the fire to burn out. Take any leftover ash outside and return it to the earth as an offering.

LUGHNASADH

Lughnasadh is one of the three harvest festivals of the year. It's a time when the sun's strength begins to recede as the year enters its darker period. During this time, many fruits and vegetables are harvested. The rituals in this section celebrate and honor Earth, the Harvest Mother, and Lugh, God of craftmanship and talent.

LUGH ABUNDANCE RITUAL

During Lughnasadh, crops are abundant. Throughout history, agriculture and harvest have been an important part of surviving the coming winter. In this ritual, you'll create a besom, enabling you to focus on the abundance of the season and to honor the God Lugh.

Ritual Setting

Altar

Tools and Supplies

FOR THE RITUAL

Festive decorations for Lughnasadh—grain, corn dolly, bread, sunflowers, calendulas

Wand or athame

Elemental representations

Deity representation for Lugh—statue, candle, image, or symbol

1 pillar candle—orange, yellow, or red

Fire-safe plate or candle holder

Lighter or matches

Cake and ale—cookies, bread, or treats and wine, cider, or water

FOR THE BESOM

30 to 50 (8-inch) bristles, twigs, or dried woody herb (mugwort or thyme)

Rubber band

Spool of string or cord

Pruning shears or boline

1 (12-inch) ribbon—orange, yellow, or red

PRIOR TO THE RITUAL

1. Shower or bathe, visualizing all old or unwanted energies leaving your being.

2. Cleanse the altar.

PREPARING THE ALTAR

Place the festive decorations and tools on the altar. Place the elemental representations in a pentacle configuration. Place the deity representation at the top of the altar. Place the candle on the fire-safe plate in the center of the pentacle, leaving enough room to work with your besom materials.

THE RITUAL

1. Cast a circle of protection. Hold the wand or athame as an extension of your hand to gather and direct energy as you call upon the elements. Starting from the east and ending north, call upon the element of air for mental clarity, the element of fire for power, the element of water for fluidity, and the element of earth for stability.

2. Invoke the God Lugh to assist you with your ritual by saying: *"Mighty Lugh, the craftsman God, a master of art, talent, and skill, join me here today to assist me with mastering this craft."*

3. Light the candle and set your intentions to show respect for Lugh and the abundance of the season.

4. Gather the bristles into a bunch and secure one end with the rubber band.

5. Pull string or twine from the spool and begin wrapping the secured end of the bristles (leave the end of the string loose so you can tie it at the end). This will become the handle of the besom. Wrap tightly until you have a 3- or 4-inch handle. Cut the string and tie it to secure.

6. Tie the ribbon to the besom's handle and say: *"Abundance besom, I tie this knot; may you carry abundance into the winter season."*

7. Portion out an offering of cake and ale. Take a sip and have a bite of your own as well.

CONTINUED

8. Thank Lugh for his presence and strength by saying: *"Mighty Lugh, I thank you for your presence here today and for lending me the strength of skill. May you go as you please and accept my offering as a token of my appreciation."*

9. Release the elements in reverse order by beginning facing the north and ending east, thanking each element for their assistance and bidding them farewell. Then open the circle by saying: *"I open this circle and release the energy back into the earth."*

10. Extinguish the candle or allow it to burn out. Cover the cake and ale and leave it on the altar overnight as an offering. The next day, dispose of it by returning it to the earth.

HARVEST MOTHER BREAD RITUAL

Grain is an important element of Lughnasadh, and leaving an offering of bread is an excellent way to honor the spirit of grain and the earth. This simple ritual calls for freshly baked bread to give back to the Harvest Mother, sometimes called the Grain Mother.

Ritual Setting
Outdoor altar and outdoors

Tools and Supplies

Festive decorations for Lughnasadh—dried grain, corn, flowers

Wand or athame

Elemental representations

Deity representation for Harvest Mother—statue, candle, image, or symbol

4 tea light candles—white or yellow

Fire-safe plates or candle holders

Freshly baked bread

Cutting board

Lighter or matches

Bread knife

Cup or chalice of wine, cider, water, or other drink of choice

PRIOR TO THE RITUAL

1. Shower or bathe, visualizing all old or unwanted energies leaving your being.

2. Prepare freshly baked bread, setting your intentions of abundance and promoting good fortune.

3. Cleanse the altar.

PREPARING THE ALTAR

Place the festive decorations and tools on the altar. Place the elemental representations in a pentacle configuration. Place the deity representation at the top of the altar. Place the candles on the fire-safe plates in a square configuration on the altar. Place the bread on the cutting board in the center of the square.

CONTINUED

THE RITUAL

1. Cast a circle of protection. Hold the wand or athame as an extension of your hand to gather and direct energy as you call upon the elements. Starting from the east and ending north, call upon the element of air for mental clarity, the element of fire for power, the element of water for fluidity, and the element of earth for stability.

2. Invoke the Harvest Mother by saying: *"Mother of the Harvest, with your abundant grain, I welcome you here today to celebrate the bountiful earth."*

3. Light the candles. Cut six slices of bread from the loaf: one slice for you, one for the Harvest Mother, and four as offerings to the earth.

4. Take a sip of your drink and a bite of bread and say: *"Fulfilled and blessed for all that I've received, Mother of the Harvest, accept this offering of bread, a gift to you in exchange for gifts yet to come. I thank you for your assistance here today."*

5. Extinguish the candles, then release the elements in reverse order by beginning facing the north and ending east, thanking each element for their assistance and bidding them farewell. Then open the circle by saying: *"I open this circle and release the energy back into the earth."*

6. Return the remaining four slices of bread to the earth as offerings, placing them at the four corners of your property.

7. Cover the bread offering to the Harvest Mother and leave it on the altar overnight. The next day, return it to the earth.

MABON

On **Mabon**, or the Autumn Equinox, the Earth experiences equal nighttime and daytime (like the Spring Equinox). It's the second of the three harvest festivals. During this time, you'll often notice a wave of fruit and vegetables being harvested and showing up in supermarkets (or even in your own garden). Mabon is an ideal time to reflect and focus on goals.

MABON ACCUMULATION RITUAL

During Mabon, the second harvest, we honor what we've reaped from the earth. It is a time to celebrate nature and all it provides. This ritual is an opportunity to write down our thanks for what the earth gives us, creating a time capsule for the Wheel of the Year.

Ritual Setting
Altar

Tools and Supplies

FOR THE RITUAL

Festive decorations for Mabon—root vegetables, apples, grapes, harvest decorations

Wand or athame

Elemental representations

Deity representation

FOR THE CAPSULE

Pen and paper

Mason jar or empty coffee can with lid

1 (4- or 5-piece) bouquet of greenery and flowers

1 clear quartz or yellow crystal—yellow agate, citrine, yellow topaz, or tiger's eye

1 ounce dried sage

PRIOR TO THE RITUAL

1. Shower or bathe, visualizing all old or unwanted energies leaving your being.

2. Cleanse the altar.

CONTINUED

PREPARING THE ALTAR

Place the decorations, tools, and supplies on the altar. Place the elemental representations in a pentacle configuration. Place the deity representation at the top of the altar.

THE RITUAL

1. Cast a circle of protection. Hold the wand or athame as an extension of your hand to gather and direct energy as you call upon the elements. Starting from the east and ending north, call upon the element of air for mental clarity, the element of fire for power, the element of water for fluidity, and the element of earth for stability.

2. Invoke the God and Goddess by saying something like: *"God and Goddess of the Mabon Harvest, I invite you to join my sacred circle."*

3. Using the pen and paper, write a letter about all that you're thankful for. Think about everything you've accumulated thus far in your life and all the earth has given you.

4. Place the letter in the jar along with the bouquet.

5. Place the crystal in the jar and sprinkle the sage on top, saying: *"I am thankful for all that I have and blessed for all my experiences. It's time to look within and celebrate all that I've accumulated."*

6. Cover the jar with its lid and thank the God and Goddess: *"God and Goddess of the Mabon Harvest, I humbly thank you for your presence here. Go if you desire or stay if you'd like."*

7. Release the elements in reverse order by beginning facing the north and ending east, thanking each element for their assistance and bidding them farewell. Then open the circle by saying: *"I open this circle and release the energy back into the earth."*

8. Bury the capsule outside. If you'd like, you can retrieve it and repeat the ritual the following year.

MABON RELEASE RITUAL

Mabon is a time to take stock of all that you have, both physically and spiritually, and to release what no longer serves you. This ritual will help you think about what it's time to let go of, as well as what might be holding you back. You'll use divination to help you get to the root of what you need to release.

Ritual Setting
Altar

Tools and Supplies

Festive decorations for Mabon

Wand or athame

Elemental representations

Deity representation

1 crystal—smoky or clear quartz

Tarot deck, Oracle deck, or other divination system

Journal and pen

Offering of choice

PRIOR TO THE RITUAL

1. Shower or bathe, visualizing all old or unwanted energies leaving your being.

2. Cleanse the altar.

PREPARING THE ALTAR

Place the festive decorations and tools on the altar. Place the elemental representations in a pentacle configuration. Place the deity representation at the top of the altar. Place the crystal and divination deck in the middle of the pentacle.

THE RITUAL

1. Cast a circle of protection. Hold the wand or athame as an extension of your hand to gather and direct energy as you call upon the elements. Starting from the east and ending north, call upon the element of air for mental clarity, the element of fire for power, the element of water for fluidity, and the element of earth for stability.

CONTINUED

2. Invoke deities by saying something like: *"Deities of Mabon, I welcome you to my sacred circle."*

3. Close your eyes and meditate for 5 to 10 minutes on your year thus far until you have a sense of what needs to be released.

4. Begin to shuffle your divination deck until you feel compelled to stop.

5. Fan out the cards on the altar. Pull three cards and ask three questions: Which area in my life is out of balance? What no longer serves me currently? How might I bring balance back to my life?

6. Spend 5 to 10 minutes reflecting on the three cards, using them to help you interpret what you need to release. Use the journal to take notes.

7. Thank the deities and leave your offering: *"Deities of Mabon, I humbly thank you for your presence here. Go if you desire or stay if you'd like."*

8. Release the elements in reverse order by beginning facing the north and ending east, thanking each element for their assistance and bidding them farewell. Then open the circle by saying: *"I open this circle and release the energy back into the earth."*

9. Leave the offering on the altar.

SAMHAIN

Samhain marks the end of the harvest season and the beginning of the darker half of the year, when the sun's energy wanes. Samhain, the halfway point to Yule or the Winter Solstice, is also a night when the veil between the physical and spiritual worlds is at its thinnest. The rituals in this section focus on honoring your ancestors and holding a "**dumb supper**"—a silent dinner to honor the deceased.

SAMHAIN ANCESTOR RITUAL

Samhain is a time to honor and pay tribute to your ancestors or deceased loved ones. This simple ritual will help you show your appreciation and share memories. It uses a purple candle for spirit communication and heirlooms to connect you to your departed loved ones or ancestors.

Ritual Setting
Altar

Tools and Supplies

Festive decorations for Samhain—flowers, crystals, or mementos

Wand or athame

Elemental representation

Deity representation

1 pillar candle—purple

1 cone or stick incense—cinnamon, clove, patchouli, rosemary, or sage

Fire-safe plates or candle holder and incense holder

Photograph or heirloom for each person you want to connect with

Lighter or matches

Bell

Offering of choice—food, craft, or something important

PRIOR TO THE RITUAL

1. Shower or bathe, visualizing all old or unwanted energies leaving your being.

2. Cleanse the altar.

CONTINUED

PREPARING THE ALTAR

Place the festive decorations and tools on the altar. Place the elemental representations in a pentacle configuration. Place the deity representation at the top of the altar. Place the candle and incense (on the fire-safe plates) and any symbols, photographs, or heirlooms of your deceased loved ones or ancestors around the altar, in positions you feel are best.

THE RITUAL

1. Cast a circle of protection. Hold the wand or athame as an extension of your hand to gather and direct energy as you call upon the elements. Starting from the east and ending north, call upon the element of air for mental clarity, the element of fire for power, the element of water for fluidity, and the element of earth for stability.

2. Invoke your chosen deity or deities by saying something like: *"Lord and Lady, I invite you to join this sacred circle."*

3. Light the candle and incense and say the name(s) of your loved one(s).

4. Ring the bell to raise energy and then say to your loved one(s): *"I call out to you to welcome, honor, and thank you. You are gone but never forgotten, for I remember. I hold close our memories together, and you will continue to live on within me."*

5. Spend time sharing memories and thanking your loved one(s) for being part of your life, silently or out loud.

6. Place the offering on the altar. Thank your loved one(s) for their presence and say your goodbyes.

7. Thank the deities for their assistance by saying: *"Lord and Lady, I humbly thank you for your presence here. Go if you desire or stay if you'd like."*

8. Release the elements in reverse order by beginning facing the north and ending east, thanking each element for their assistance and bidding them farewell. Then open the circle by saying: *"I open this circle and release the energy back into the earth."*

9. Extinguish the candle and incense. Leave the offering on the altar.

DUMB SUPPER

A "dumb supper" refers to a silent dinner or "feast to the dead" at which a seat must be provided for the deceased. This ritual involves eating a meal, writing letters to the deceased, and burning the letters in a fireplace or fire-safe cauldron. The ritual should be conducted in complete silence.

Ritual Setting

Dining room table or area where food can be served

Tools and Supplies

Festive decorations for Samhain—black décor is traditional but not required

Photographs or heirlooms of the deceased

Festive food, drink, and place settings for each guest

Wand or athame

Elemental representations

Deity representation

Taper or votive candles for each place setting—white, purple, or black

Fire-safe plates or candle holders

Pens and paper, for guests to write letters

Lighter or matches

Bell

Fireplace or fire-safe cauldron

PRIOR TO RITUAL

1. Shower or bathe, visualizing all old or unwanted energies leaving your being. Wear black or festive clothing for this event.

2. Cleanse the altar.

PREPARING THE ALTAR

Decorate the room and place the decorations and photographs or mementos of the deceased on your dining table. Set a place setting for each guest, including one for the deceased. Prepare the food and drink. Position the elemental and deity representations around the room. Place the candles on fire-safe plates on the table, one for each person, including the deceased guests. If you will be calling multiple spirits, place the equivalent number of candles at the empty place setting. Once the guests arrive, have each guest write a letter to the spirit they wish to commune with and bring their letter to their place setting.

THE RITUAL

1. Silently cast a circle of protection to call upon the elements. Hold the wand or athame as an extension of your hand to gather and direct energy.

2. Invoke the deity silently by closing your eyes and willing the assistance of the God and Goddess.

3. Serve the food and drink, light the candles, and ring the bell to shift the energy in the room, commencing the celebration.

4. Eat in silence, spending the time thinking about your departed loved ones and the messages you wrote.

5. At the end of the feast, help the guests burn their letters in a fire-safe cauldron or fireplace. Burn your own letter as well.

6. After all the letters have been burned, ring the bell again to end the supper.

7. Silently thank the God and Goddess for watching over the feast.

8. Silently release the elements, open the circle, and extinguish the candles and any embers in the fireplace or cauldron.

9. The room should remain silent. If you wish to speak, you may leave the room and converse elsewhere or dismiss your guests and end the supper.

CHAPTER 6
MOON CELEBRATIONS (ESBATS)

Along with the eight sabbats, or solar celebrations, Wiccans also celebrate and observe the 12 (or 13) **esbats**, or full moon celebrations. Since the 12-month calendar does not sync perfectly with astronomical events, the year occasionally has a thirteenth moon (a second moon in a single month), which is sometimes called a **blue moon**.

Some Wiccans use the **Celtic Tree calendar**, which consists of 13 lunar divisions with fixed dates. These 13 lunar months are named after trees and are based on the Celtic Ogham (*oh-wam*) alphabet. Other Wiccans use the **Gregorian calendar** (the 365.4245-day calendar used by most of the modern world). Regardless of the calendar you follow, each full moon contains potent energy that you can use to power spellwork, meditate, charge ritual items, commune with a deity, and even complete divination rituals. The following esbat rituals are divided by the month they fall in according to the Gregorian calendar, but I've also included the corresponding date ranges for those Wiccans who work with the Celtic Tree calendar. You can perform these esbat rituals when the full moon lands anywhere within the provided date ranges, celebrating the corresponding moon.

Esbats are most powerful when they are performed outside during the full moon, weather permitting. They can also be performed during the evening after the sun has set. Try to make it outside during the warmer months, but if you can't, performing esbats indoors is perfectly acceptable. If performing indoors, try to include extra moon imagery, charms, or even a candle to represent the energy of the full moon. During indoor esbats, you can also use oils or **full moon charged water** to anoint your forehead. To make full moon charged water, leave a bowl of water overnight under the light of the full moon.

When celebrating an esbat, you'll frequently invoke the Goddess (as opposed to the God). Many Wiccans choose to incorporate the season when choosing a Goddess or pantheon—for example, Mother for balanced winter and summer, Maiden for fertile spring, and Crone for aging autumn. You can choose which deity you work with; practitioners sometimes invoke both the God and Goddess.

These rituals are designed mostly for solitary Wiccans, but each ritual can be adapted for a group or coven. To alter the ritual, divide the steps amongst the group.

JANUARY MOON

Gregorian Calendar: The January moon is often called the wolf, cold, or ice moon. During this full moon, work on magic regarding protection and developing your inner self, intuition, and wisdom.

Celtic Tree Calendar: This time period includes the Birch moon, celebrated from December 24 to January 20, and the Rowan moon, celebrated from January 21 to February 17. The Celtic name for *birch* is *beth*, pronounced *beh*, and the name for the *rowan* is *Luis*, pronounced *loush*. The Birch moon is associated with new beginnings, rebirth, regeneration, protection, and puri-fication, and the Rowan moon is associated with new life, strength, success, and the Celtic Goddess Brigid.

REBIRTH MEDITATION ESBAT

During the Winter Solstice in December, the sun begins its slow return to strength. With the sun's return comes light, new beginnings, regen-eration, and rebirth. This ritual focuses on harnessing this strong energy and honoring the cycle of life through meditation.

Ritual Setting
Altar

Tools and Supplies

Wand or athame

Elemental representations—candles, symbolic items, or symbols written on stone or wood

Deity representation for Moon Goddess—statue, candle, or image

3 votive or pillar candles—white

1 cone or stick incense—lotus, lavender, frankincense, or anise

Fire-safe plates or candle holders and incense holder

Device to play meditation or relaxation music

Lighter or matches

Offering of choice

CONTINUED

PRIOR TO THE RITUAL

1. Shower or bathe, visualizing all old or unwanted energies leaving your being.

2. Cleanse the altar.

PREPARING THE ALTAR

Place the tools and supplies on the altar. Place the elemental representations in a pentacle configuration. Place the deity representation at the top of the altar. Place the candles on fire-safe plates and the incense in a holder in front of you on the altar, however you see fit.

THE RITUAL

1. Cast a circle of protection. Hold the wand or athame as an extension of your hand to gather and direct energy as you call upon elements. Starting from the east and ending north, call upon the element of air for mental clarity, the element of fire for power, the element of water for fluidity, and the element of earth for stability.

2. Turn on the music. Sit comfortably in front of the altar. Light the candles and incense.

3. Invoke the Goddess of the Moon to assist you with your ritual: *"Goddess of the Moon, Crone of Winter, I ask for your guidance tonight. As I journey within, lend me your strength and illuminate my path."*

4. Close your eyes and take a few deep breaths. Allow yourself to become relaxed. Visualize yourself walking under the moonlight, basking in its glow. Allow yourself to feel the energy of the Goddess of the Moon surrounding you. As moonlight envelopes your being, imagine you're transforming and beginning anew for the year ahead.

5. Allow yourself to stay in this space as long as you'd like. When you're ready, walk back along the mental path you traveled until you're back where you started.

6. Thank the deity and leave your offering: *"Goddess of the Moon, Crone of Winter, I thank you for your assistance tonight. Accept my offering and gratitude."*

7. Release the elements in reverse order by beginning facing the north and ending east, thanking each element for their assistance and bidding them farewell. Then open the circle by saying: *"I open this circle and release the energy back into the earth."*

8. Snuff out the incense and candles. Leave the offering on the altar.

PROTECTION CHARM ESBAT

In Wiccan practice, a major theme in the month of January is protection. In this ritual, you'll craft a protection charm bag using January's strong lunar energy. You can carry this charm with you wherever you go as a form of protection.

Ritual Setting
Altar

Tools and Supplies

FOR THE RITUAL

Wand or athame

Elemental representations

Deity representation for
  Moon Goddess

Offering of choice

FOR THE CHARM BAG

Drawstring pouch

1 ounce dried basil

2 dried bay leaves

6 whole cloves

1 cinnamon stick

1 crystal—hematite or obsidian

PRIOR TO THE RITUAL

1. Shower or bathe, visualizing all old or unwanted energies leaving your being.

2. Cleanse the altar.

PREPARING THE ALTAR

Place the tools and supplies on the altar. Place the elemental representations in a pentacle configuration. Place the deity representations at the top of the altar.

THE RITUAL

1. Cast a circle of protection. Hold the wand or athame as an extension of your hand to gather and direct energy as you call upon the elements. Starting from the east and ending north, call upon the element of air for mental clarity, the element of fire for power, the element of water for fluidity, and the element of earth for stability.

2. Invoke the Moon Goddess by saying something like: *"Lunar Goddess, I invite you to my sacred circle. Grant me your blessings and energy tonight."*

3. Open the drawstring pouch and add the basil, bay leaves, cloves, cinnamon stick, and crystal, pausing to set your intentions to protect as you add each item.

4. Once finished, say: *"Charm of protection, infuse with the light of the moon and charge with protection energy, so that I may be free from all worry."*

5. Tie the pouch shut to complete the charm bag.

6. Thank the deity by saying: *"Lunar Goddess, I thank you for your assistance and presence tonight."*

7. Release the elements in reverse order by beginning facing the north and ending east, thanking each element for their assistance and bidding them farewell. Then open the circle by saying: *"I open this circle and release the energy back into the earth."*

8. Leave the offering for the Moon Goddess on the altar.

9. Place the charm bag under moonlight to further charge it with energy. Carry the bag with you when you need protection.

FEBRUARY MOON

Gregorian Calendar: The February moon is often called the quickening, snow, hunger, chaste, or cleansing moon. During this full moon, work on magic related to purification, growth, love, and healing.

Celtic Tree Calendar: The Rowan moon is celebrated until February 17, and the Ash moon is celebrated from February 18 to March 17. The Celtic name for *ash* is *nion*, pronounced *knee-un*. The Rowan moon is associated with new life, strength, and success, and the Ash moon is associated with healing, strength, and endurance.

PURIFICATION ESBAT

Purification works by using the energy of the full moon to expel tiredness, sadness, and the effects of negativity. This ritual is stronger than an average purification or cleansing because it involves communing with the Moon Goddess in addition to using your own energy.

Ritual Setting
Altar

Tools and Supplies

Wand or athame

Elemental representations—incense for air, candle for fire, bowl of water, and a crystal for earth

Deity representation for Moon Goddess

Offering of choice—cake and ale, foraged items, or a crafted gift

Any new ritual objects that need purification (optional)

PRIOR TO THE RITUAL

1. Shower or bathe, visualizing all old or unwanted energies leaving your being.

2. Cleanse the altar.

PREPARING THE ALTAR

Place the tools and supplies on the altar. Place the elemental representations in a pentacle configuration. Place the deity representation at the top of the altar. If you are purifying any ritual objects, place them on the altar as well.

THE RITUAL

1. Cast a circle of protection. Hold the wand or athame as an extension of your hand to gather and direct energy as you call upon the elements. Starting from the east and ending north, call upon the element of air for mental clarity, the element of fire for power, the element of water for fluidity, and the element of earth for stability.

2. Invoke the Moon Goddess by saying: *"I call upon the Goddess of the Moon. Please join my circle and guide me with your light."*

3. Visualize the moon's light mixing with your own light. Let it envelop your being. Chant to the Goddess: *"Goddess of the Moon, lend me your power to cleanse and purify on this esbat rite."* Visualize and feel yourself becoming lighter, free of stress and negativity.

4. Once you feel the positive effects of purification, thank the Moon Goddess by saying: *"Great Goddess of the Moon, I thank you for your presence. Accept my offering for your assistance tonight."*

5. Place the offering on the altar in front of the deity representation.

6. Release the elements in reverse order by beginning facing the north and ending east, thanking each element for their assistance and bidding them farewell. Then open the circle by saying: *"I open this circle and release the energy back into the earth."*

7. If the offering contains food, cover it. Leave the offering on the altar overnight.

8. If you are purifying ritual items, place them by a window or outside to charge under the light of the full moon.

HEALING ESBAT

The February moon has powerful healing energy that you can tap into during a healing esbat. You can perform this ritual on yourself or a loved one who needs assistance with healing. An important note: Before performing a ritual on anyone other than yourself, make sure you have their consent.

Ritual Setting
Altar

Tools and Supplies

Wand or athame

Elemental representations

Deity representation

1 votive or pillar candle—blue (for healing)

Fire-safe plate or candle holder

Photograph of or item belonging to the person who needs healing

Lighter or matches

1 ounce dried lavender

1 ounce dried rosemary

Offering of choice

PRIOR TO THE RITUAL

1. Shower or bathe, visualizing all old or unwanted energies leaving your being.

2. Cleanse the altar.

PREPARING THE ALTAR

Place the tools and supplies on the altar. Place the elemental representations in a pentacle configuration. Place the deity representation at the top of the altar. Place the candle on the fire-safe plate in the center of the altar. In front of the candle, place the photograph or item.

THE RITUAL

1. Cast a circle of protection. Hold the wand or athame as an extension of your hand to gather and direct energy as you call upon the elements. Starting from the east and ending north, call upon the element of air for mental clarity, the element of fire for power, the element of water for fluidity, and the element of earth for stability.

2. Invoke your deities of choice by saying something like: *"Lord and Lady, I invite you to join my sacred circle tonight."*

3. Light the candle and state your intentions for healing.

4. Hold up the photograph or item. Describe the ailment out loud.

5. Sprinkle the lavender and rosemary onto the candle's flame and say: *"Healing herbs, I invoke your power: rosemary for promoting recovery, lavender for easing pain."*

6. Meditate for 10 to 20 minutes, focusing on the person who is ailing.

7. When you are ready, thank the deities and leave your offering: *"Lord and Lady, I thank you for your presence and guidance tonight."* Snuff out the candle.

8. Release the elements in reverse order by beginning facing the north and ending east, thanking each element for their assistance and bidding them farewell. Then open the circle by saying: *"I open this circle and release the energy back into the earth."*

9. Relight the candle every night to bring about more healing energy.

MARCH MOON

Gregorian Calendar: The March moon is often called the storm, seed, grass, rain, worm, or hunger moon. During this full moon, you can work on magic relating to rebirth, prosperity, fertility, cleansing, balance, and growth.

Celtic Tree Calendar: The Ash moon is celebrated until March 17, and the Alder moon is celebrated from March 18 to April 14. The Celtic name for *alder* is *fearn*, pronounced *fairin*. The Ash moon is associated with healing, strength, and endurance, and the Alder moon is associated with courage, strength, intuition, and spirituality.

GROWTH ESBAT

During March, life is growing and bursting from the earth, and the full moons promote growth and nurturing energy. March is the month of the Spring Equinox, when equal parts of night and day bring balance. This ritual uses salt as a representation of Earth to promote balance, positivity, and growth.

Ritual Setting
Altar

Tools and Supplies

Wand or athame

Elemental representations

Deity representation

Cauldron

Small bowl of salt

Bowl of water

Offering of choice—food, foraged
   items, or crafts

PRIOR TO THE RITUAL

1. Shower or bathe, visualizing all old or unwanted energies leaving your being.

2. Cleanse the altar.

PREPARING THE ALTAR

Place the tools and supplies on the altar. Place the elemental representations in a pentacle configuration. Place the deity representation at the top of the altar. Place the cauldron, salt, and bowl of water at the center of the altar.

THE RITUAL

1. Cast a circle of protection. Hold the wand or athame as an extension of your hand to gather and direct energy as you call upon the elements. Starting from the east and ending north, call upon the element of air for mental clarity, the element of fire for power, the element of water for fluidity, and the element of earth for stability.

2. Invite your deities: *"Deities of the March moon, I ask for your assistance and guidance tonight."*

3. Sprinkle the salt into the cauldron and say: *"Salt of Earth, I invoke your energy. Bring me balance and peace of mind and imbue me with growth and positivity under the light of the full moon."*

4. Pour the water over the salt and say: *"Water of life, I invoke your energy. Bring me nourishing energy and life and infuse me with growth and positivity under the light of the full moon."*

5. Thank the deities and leave your offering: *"Deities of the March moon, I thank you for your presence tonight."*

6. Release the elements in reverse order by beginning facing the north and ending east, thanking each element for their assistance and bidding them farewell. Then open the circle by saying: *"I open this circle and release the energy back into the earth."*

7. Dispose of the saltwater outside, away from plants or other greenery (salt can dehydrate and kill plants).

HOME CLEANSING ESBAT

March is a time for spring cleaning to refresh our environments after the long winter. This home ritual wash uses the energy of the full moon, the cleansing power of water, and the **Laguz rune**, which represents the renewing energy of water.

Ritual Setting

Kitchen and home

Tools and Supplies

Wand or athame

Elemental representations

Deity representation

Bucket

Wash mixture

Sponge

Drying cloth

Laguz runestone, or other visual reference of Laguz

Offering of choice—food or foraged or crafted item

FOR THE WASH MIXTURE

2 liters water

½ cup vinegar

10 drops lavender essential oil

10 drops sage essential oil

10 drops lemon or orange essential oil

PRIOR TO THE RITUAL

1. Shower or bathe, visualizing all old or unwanted energies leaving your being.

2. Cleanse the kitchen.

PREPARING THE ALTAR

Set up a space in your kitchen where you can easily access the supplies for this ritual. Place the elemental representations wherever you feel is best around your kitchen. In a bucket, combine the water, vinegar, and essential oils to create the wash.

THE RITUAL

1. Cast a circle of protection. Hold the wand or athame as an extension of your hand to gather and direct energy as you call upon the elements. Starting from the east and ending north, call upon the element of air for mental clarity, the element of fire for power, the element of water for fluidity, and the element of earth for stability.

2. Invoke the God and Goddess or deity of your choice by saying something like: *"God and Goddess, I invite you to my sacred circle tonight."*

3. Using the sponge and drying cloth, begin cleaning your home with the wash. Focus on any entrances, including windows and even chimneys or vents. Of course, do not use the wash in areas that could be damaged by water.

4. Dip your finger into the wash and draw the Laguz rune on your windows. This will instill its renewing energy into your home.

5. When you are ready, leave your offering and thank your deity of choice: *"God and Goddess, I thank you for your presence tonight."*

6. Release the elements in reverse order by beginning facing the north and ending east, thanking each element for their assistance and bidding them farewell. Then open the circle by saying: *"I open this circle and release the energy back into the earth."*

7. Discard any remaining ritual wash mixture.

APRIL MOON

Gregorian Calendar: The April moon is often called the wind, hare, planting, or pink moon. During this full moon, work on magic relating to change, emotions, planning, and new beginnings.

Celtic Tree Calendar: The Alder moon is celebrated until April 14 and the Willow moon is celebrated from April 15 to May 12. The Celtic name for *willow* is *saille*, pronounced *sahl-yeh*. The Alder moon is associated with courage, strength, enhancing your intuition and spirituality, and the Willow moon is associated with flexibility, knowledge, protection, and intuition.

EMPOWERING CHANGE ESBAT

This ritual will assist you in creating positive change in your life. Change can teach us flexibility, reveal our strength, and open up new opportunities. In this ritual, you will use divination, green crystals (representing transformation and change), and the energy of the full moon to guide you in interpreting messages.

Ritual Setting
Altar

Tools and Supplies

Wand or athame

Elemental representations

Deity representation

Tarot deck, Oracle deck,
  or other divination system

3 green crystals—malachite,
  chrysoprase, or amazonite

Lighter or matches

1 cone or stick incense—cinnamon,
  mugwort, rose, or jasmine

Fire-safe plate or incense holder

Journal and pen

Offering of choice

PRIOR TO THE RITUAL

1. Shower or bathe, visualizing all old or unwanted energies leaving your being.

2. Cleanse the altar.

PREPARING THE ALTAR

Place the tools and supplies on the altar. Place the elemental representations in a pentacle configuration. Place the deity representation at the top of the altar. Place the divination deck and crystals in the center of the pentacle.

THE RITUAL

1. Cast a circle of protection. Hold the wand or athame as an extension of your hand to gather and direct energy as you call upon the elements. Starting from the east and ending north, call upon the element of air for mental clarity, the element of fire for power, the element of water for fluidity, and the element of earth for stability.

2. Invoke the God and Goddess or deity of your choice by saying something like: *"Goddess of the Moon, Maiden of Spring, I invite you to my circle tonight."*

3. Light the incense on a fire-safe plate and set your intentions to invite change into your life.

4. Shuffle the divination deck until you feel compelled to stop.

5. Fan out the cards on the altar. Pull three cards and ask three questions: Which area of my life most needs change? What action needs to take place in order to change? What will I gain from making these changes?

6. Spend 5 to 10 minutes reflecting on the three cards, using them to help you interpret what you need to change. Use the journal to take notes.

CONTINUED

7. Place your offering on the altar and thank the deity: *"Goddess of the Moon, Maiden of Spring, I thank you for your presence tonight."*

8. Release the elements in reverse order by beginning facing the north and ending east, thanking each element for their assistance and bidding them farewell. Then open the circle by saying: *"I open this circle and release the energy back into the earth."*

9. Extinguish the incense or allow it to burn out. Leave the offering on the altar.

INTENTIONS AND MANIFESTATION ESBAT

The act of planning can make a big difference in your life by giving you control over your future. With this planning esbat ritual, you use the energy of the moon to help you set your intentions and manifest the change you want in your life. This ritual also uses meditation as part of the process of manifesting change.

Ritual Setting

Altar

Tools and Supplies

Wand or athame

Elemental representations

Deity representation

Lighter or matches

1 cone or stick incense—
  frankincense, lavender,
  sandalwood, or dragon's blood

Fire-safe plate or incense holder

Journal and pen

Offering of choice—food,
  foraged items, or crafts

PRIOR TO THE RITUAL

1. Shower or bathe, visualizing all old or unwanted energies leaving your being.

2. Cleanse the altar.

PREPARING THE ALTAR

Place the tools and supplies on the altar. Place the elemental representations in a pentacle configuration. Place the deity representation at the top of the altar. Position the rest of your items in the center of the pentacle.

CONTINUED

THE RITUAL

1. Cast a circle of protection. Hold the wand or athame as an extension of your hand to gather and direct energy as you call upon the elements. Starting from the east and ending north, call upon the element of air for mental clarity, the element of fire for power, the element of water for fluidity, and the element of earth for stability.

2. Invoke the God and Goddess or deity of your choice by saying something like: *"Great Lord and Lady, grant me your blessings and guidance tonight."*

3. Light the incense on the fire-safe plate and set your intentions for the ritual to be guided.

4. Meditate for 5 to 10 minutes to calm your mind. Allow yourself to be led by your heart and desires.

5. Once you have finished meditating, write in the journal about your thoughts, ideas, desires, and goals. Allow yourself to dream big and dig deep within to access the things you want to manifest in your life.

6. When you've finished writing, thank the deities: *"Great Lord and Lady, I thank you for your presence tonight."*

7. Place the offering on the altar.

8. Release the elements in reverse order by beginning facing the north and ending east, thanking each element for their assistance and bidding them farewell. Then open the circle by saying: *"I open this circle and release the energy back into the earth."*

9. Extinguish the incense or allow it to burn out. Leave the offering on the altar.

MAY MOON

Gregorian Calendar: The May moon is often called the flower, hare, milk, planting, or merry moon. During this full moon, work on magic relating to passion, building energy, and trusting your intuition.

Celtic Tree Calendar: The Willow moon is celebrated until May 12 and the Hawthorn moon is celebrated from May 13 to June 9. The Celtic name for hawthorn is *huath,* pronounced *hoh-uh.* The Willow moon is associated with flexibility, knowledge, protection, and intuition, and the Hawthorn moon is associated with protection, energy, connections, hope, and pleasure.

ENERGY BUILDING ESBAT

With this esbat, you can harness the potency of the moon to build up your energy. In this ritual, you'll create a charged bottle of oil that you can use on pressure points on your skin to boost your energy. Prior to use, test the oil on a small patch of skin on the inside of your elbow to make sure it doesn't irritate you.

Ritual Setting
Altar

Tools and Supplies

Wand or athame

Elemental representations

Deity representation

Offering of choice—food, herbs, flowers, or crystals

FOR THE OIL

1 (2-ounce) glass dropper or roller bottle

2 ounces skincare carrier oil—jojoba, olive, or apricot kernel

3 drops eucalyptus essential oil

4 drops peppermint essential oil

5 drops rosemary essential oil

PRIOR TO THE RITUAL

1. Shower or bathe, visualizing all old or unwanted energies leaving your being.

2. Cleanse the altar.

CONTINUED

PREPARING THE ALTAR

Place the tools and supplies on the altar. Place the elemental representations in a pentacle configuration. Place the deity representation at the top of the altar. Place the carrier and essential oils in the center of the pentacle.

THE RITUAL

1. Cast a circle of protection. Hold the wand or athame as an extension of your hand to gather and direct energy as you call upon the elements. Starting from the east and ending north, call upon the element of air for mental clarity, the element of fire for power, the element of water for fluidity, and the element of earth for stability.

2. Invoke the Moon Goddess by saying something like: *"Goddess of the Flower Moon, Maiden of the Night, please join me on this beautiful May evening, and illuminate this esbat rite."*

3. Pour the carrier oil into the glass bottle until it is full. Then add the eucalyptus, peppermint, and rosemary essential oils one at a time.

4. Hold the bottle in your hands and say: *"Oil, now infused, charge, and grant me energy as strong as the moon for the coming days."*

5. Thank the Moon Goddess and leave your offering: *"Goddess of the Flower Moon, Maiden of the Night, I thank you for your assistance tonight and leave you this offering."*

6. Release the elements in reverse order by beginning facing the north and ending east, thanking each element for their assistance and bidding them farewell. Then open the circle by saying: *"I open this circle and release the energy back into the earth."*

7. Leave the offering on the altar. Wear the oil whenever you need an energy boost.

CONNECTIONS ESBAT

Strengthening your connections with others is an important part of any healthy, long-lasting relationship. This ritual combines visualization techniques with full moon energy and a red candle to represent love.

Ritual Setting
Altar

Tools and Supplies

Wand or athame

Elemental representations

Deity representation

1 pillar or votive candle—red

Fire-safe plate or candle holder

1 rose or handful of dried rose petals

Lighter or matches

PRIOR TO THE RITUAL

1. Shower or bathe, visualizing all old or unwanted energies leaving your being.

2. Cleanse the altar.

PREPARING THE ALTAR

Place the tools and supplies on the altar. Place the elemental representations in a pentacle configuration. Place the deity representation at the top of the altar. Place the candle on the fire-safe plate in the center of the pentacle. Decorate the altar with the rose petals, focusing on your intentions.

THE RITUAL

1. Cast a circle of protection. Hold the wand or athame as an extension of your hand to gather and direct energy as you call upon the elements.

2. Turn to the east and say: *"Guardian of air, I welcome you to my circle of appreciation."*

CONTINUED

3. Turn to the south and say: *"Guardian of fire, I welcome you to my circle of appreciation."*

4. Turn to the west and say: *"Guardian of water, I welcome you to my circle of appreciation."*

5. Return to the north and say: *"Guardian of earth, I welcome you to my circle of appreciation. With these elements, together with spirit, I cast a circle of protection above, below, within."*

6. Invoke the God and Goddess or deity of your choice by saying something like: *"Goddess of the May Moon, I invite you to my circle tonight. Grant me your blessings and guidance."*

7. Light the red candle and say: *"Candle of love, burn and empower, fuel my connections and strengthen my bonds."*

8. Close your eyes and visualize the candle's red energy wrapping around your body, infusing you with its energy.

9. Thank the deities by saying: *"Goddess of the May Moon, I thank you for your presence tonight."*

10. Release the elements in reverse order by beginning facing the north and ending east, thanking each element for their assistance and bidding them farewell. Then open the circle by saying: *"I open this circle and release the energy back into the earth."*

11. Extinguish the candle or allow it to burn out. Take the rose petals outside and return them to the earth as an offering.

JUNE MOON

Gregorian Calendar: The June moon is often called the strong sun moon, honey or mead moon, or strawberry moon. During this full moon, work on magic relating to protection, strength, prevention, and endurance.

Celtic Tree Calendar: The Hawthorn moon is celebrated until June 9 and the Oak moon is celebrated from June 10 to July 7. The Celtic name for *oak* is *duir,* pronounced *doo-r.* The Hawthorn moon is associated with protection, energy, connections, hope, and pleasure, and the Oak moon is associated with cleansing, strength, self-confidence, and optimism.

STRENGTHENING BATH RITUAL ESBAT

Strength is a common theme for the June moon because the days are long and the sun is strong during the time surrounding the Summer Solstice. This ritual combines the energy of the full moon with milk and honey to help you strengthen yourself physically, mentally, and spiritually.

Ritual Setting
Kitchen (to prepare) and bathroom

Tools and Supplies
Wand or athame

Elemental representations

Deity representation

Offering of choice—food, crafts, flowers, or crystals

FOR THE BATH MIXTURE

Small pot

1 cup water

1 cup honey

Wooden mixing spoon

2 cups milk

FOR THE BATH

½ cup sea salt

3 tablespoons baking soda

Bath mixture

CONTINUED

PRIOR TO THE RITUAL

1. Cleanse the ritual areas.

2. In the small pot on the stove, bring the water to a boil.

3. Once the water is boiling, pour in the honey and use the wooden spoon to stir to dissolve.

4. Pour in the milk and stir thoroughly.

5. Take the bath mixture to the bathroom. Fill the bathtub and add the salt and baking soda.

PREPARING THE ALTAR

Place the elemental and deity representations in the corners of the bathroom.

THE RITUAL

1. Cast a circle of protection. Hold the wand or athame as an extension of your hand to gather and direct energy as you call upon the elements. Starting from the east and ending north, call upon the element of air for mental clarity, the element of fire for power, the element of water for fluidity, and the element of earth for stability.

2. Invoke the deities of your choice by saying something like: *"I call upon the God and I call upon the Goddess; join my sacred space under the full moon."*

3. Add the bath mixture to the bathtub.

4. Step into the bath and breathe deeply. As you breathe, visualize strengthening energy enveloping your being. Bathe for as long as you desire.

5. When you have finished, thank the deities: *"Great God and Goddess, I thank you for your assistance tonight."*

6. Release the elements in reverse order by beginning facing the north and ending east, thanking each element for their assistance and bidding them farewell. Then open the circle by saying: *"I open this circle and release the energy back into the earth."*

7. Drain the bathtub. Leave your offering in the ritual space overnight.

STRONG SUN BONFIRE ESBAT

This ritual focuses on building energy and harnessing the strength of the June (or strong sun) moon to honor the moon and deities of choice. In this ritual, you'll create ornaments out of salt dough as an offering to deity. Making these ornaments is an opportunity to let your creativity shine.

Ritual Setting

Kitchen (to prepare) and outdoors under moonlight

Tools and Supplies

Wand or athame

Elemental representations

Deity representation

Firepit or outdoor bonfire area

Materials to start a fire (e.g., fire starter kit, petroleum jelly, wood, charcoal, lighter or matches)

Salt dough ornaments

FOR THE SALT DOUGH ORNAMENTS

Large mixing bowl

Wooden mixing spoon

2 cups all-purpose flour

½ cup table salt

¾ cup warm water

2 large pieces parchment paper

Rolling pin

Cookie cutters

Baking sheet

PRIOR TO THE RITUAL

1. Prepare the salt dough ornaments.

   ➤ Preheat the oven to 300°F.

   ➤ In the mixing bowl, combine the flour and salt. Add the warm water to the mixture in small increments. Continue stirring until the mixture begins to form a dough.

   ➤ Knead until the dough is soft, 3 to 5 minutes.

   ➤ Place the dough between the pieces of parchment paper. With the rolling pin, roll the dough until it is about ¼-inch thick. Remove the top sheet of parchment paper.

   ➤ Use cookie cutters to cut out shapes. Peel away the excess dough and transfer the parchment with the ornament shapes to the baking sheet.

   ➤ Repeat the process to use up the excess dough.

   ➤ Bake the shapes for 1 hour or until the dough has hardened completely.

2. While the ornaments are baking, shower or bathe, visualizing all old or unwanted energies leaving your being.

3. Find an outdoor space to use as a firepit or bonfire area. Cleanse the area.

PREPARING THE ALTAR

Place the tools and supplies on the outside altar. Place the elemental and deity representations intuitively around the altar space.

THE RITUAL

1. Cast a circle of protection. Hold the wand or athame as an extension of your hand to gather and direct energy as you call upon the elements. Starting from the east and ending north, call upon the element of air for mental clarity, the element of fire for power, the element of water for fluidity, and the element of earth for stability.

2. Create a small bonfire or dig a small firepit and ignite a fire. Invoke the God and Goddess or deity of your choice by saying something like: *"Lord of the Summer Sun, Lady of the Summer Moon, I invite you to my sacred circle tonight."*

3. Spend 10 to 20 minutes dancing around the flames, meditating, or gazing into the fire. Let yourself be free—this is your time to celebrate as you wish.

4. Throw some of your ornament offerings into the flames and say: *"Lord of the Summer Sun, Lady of the Summer Moon, accept this offering of love and devotion, bless me with warmth and energy, and share with me your strength and endurance."*

5. Thank the deities by saying: *"Lord of the Summer Sun, Lady of the Summer Moon, I thank you for your presence tonight."*

6. Release the elements in reverse order by beginning facing the north and ending east, thanking each element for their assistance and bidding them farewell. Then open the circle by saying: *"I open this circle and release the energy back into the earth."*

7. Safely extinguish the fire. If you have ornaments left over, you can use them to decorate your indoor altar or bury them as an offering to the earth.

JULY MOON

Gregorian Calendar: The July moon is often called the blessing, wort, hay, thunder, or buck moon. During this full moon, work on magic relating to divination, dreamwork, and psychic abilities.

Celtic Tree Calendar: The Oak moon is celebrated until July 7 and the Holly moon is celebrated from July 8 to August 4. The Celtic name for *holly* is *tinne*, pronounced *chihnn-uh*. The Oak moon is associated with cleansing, strength, self-confidence, and optimism, and the Holly moon is associated with beauty, protection, luck, and dreams.

DIVINE BLESSINGS ESBAT

July's full moon is an ideal time to slow down and reflect, and it's also useful for rituals involving blessings. This ritual, which can be performed outdoors under moonlight, will help you create a bowl of water and stone charged by the energy of the full moon.

Ritual Setting
Altar or outdoors under the full moon

Tools and Supplies

Wand or athame

Elemental representations

Deity representation

1 moonstone, or other white crystal or stone

1 pillar or votive candle—silver or white (to represent the moon)

Fire-safe plate or candle holder

Bowl of water

Lighter or matches

Offering of choice—baked goods, crafts, or foraged items

PRIOR TO THE RITUAL

1. Shower or bathe, visualizing all old or unwanted energies leaving your being.

2. Cleanse the ritual areas.

CONTINUED

PREPARING THE ALTAR

Place the tools and supplies on the altar. Place the elemental representations in a pentacle configuration. Place the deity representation at the top of the altar. Place the crystal, candle (on the fire-safe plate), and bowl of water in the center of the pentacle.

THE RITUAL

1. Cast a circle of protection. Hold the wand or athame as an extension of your hand to gather and direct energy as you call upon the elements. Starting from the east and ending north, call upon the element of air for mental clarity, the element of fire for power, the element of water for fluidity, and the element of earth for stability.

2. Invoke the God and Goddess or deity of your choice by saying something like: *"Goddess of the Blessing Moon, I invite you to my circle tonight."*

3. Light the candle and say: *"Great Moon Goddess, Queen of the Night, help illuminate my path and light my way forward into the future."*

4. Place the moonstone in the bowl of water and lift it up, saying: *"Blessing Moon, bringer of the light that shines on the earth tonight, I honor you with this water symbol of the changing tides. I cherish your insight, love, and light."*

5. Take a few moments to allow yourself to feel the energy of the moon. Meditate on your achievements and what you still want to achieve this year.

6. Thank the deity and leave your offering: *"Goddess of the Blessing Moon, I thank you for your presence tonight. I hope you accept my offering. Go if you must or stay if you'd like."*

7. Release the elements in reverse order by beginning facing the north and ending east, thanking each element for their assistance and bidding them farewell. Then open the circle by saying: *"I open this circle and release the energy back into the earth."*

8. Extinguish the candle. Leave the offering on the altar. Leave the bowl of water with the moonstone under the full moon overnight. The water and stone will be charged by the full moon.

DREAM SCRYING ESBAT

In July, you can use the full moon's energy for scrying and enhancing your psychic abilities. Scrying, discussed on page 41, involves gazing into an object or surface with unfocused eyes, allowing you to reach a state of perception where you can receive images or messages.

Ritual Setting
Altar or outdoors under the full moon

Tools and Supplies

Wand or athame

Elemental representations

Deity representation

Dark bowl filled with water

3 pillar or votive candles—silver or white (to represent the moon)

1 cone or stick incense—frankincense, lavender, rose, or jasmine

Fire-safe plates or candle holders and incense holder

Device to play meditation or relaxation music

Lighter or matches

Journal and pen

Offering of choice—baked goods, crafts, or foraged items

PRIOR TO THE RITUAL

1. Shower or bathe, visualizing all old or unwanted energies leaving your being.

2. Cleanse the ritual areas.

PREPARING THE ALTAR

Place the tools and supplies on the altar. Place the elemental representations in a pentacle configuration. Place the deity representation at the top of the altar. Place the bowl of water in the center of the pentacle. Place the candles and incense on fire-safe plates intuitively around the altar space.

THE RITUAL

1. Cast a circle of protection. Hold the wand or athame as an extension of your hand to gather and direct energy as you call upon the elements. Starting from the east and ending north, call upon the element of air for mental clarity, the element of fire for power, the element of water for fluidity, and the element of earth for stability.

2. Invoke the God and Goddess or deity of your choice by saying something like: *"Goddess of the July Moon, I invite you to my circle tonight."*

3. Turn on the music. Sit comfortably in front of the altar. Light the candles and incense.

4. Begin scrying by closing your eyes and allowing yourself to feel the energy around you.

5. Open your eyes and say: *"Water of wisdom and insight, show me the mysteries of the moon."*

6. Stare into the bowl of water. Look for patterns, symbols, or images. Write down what you see. Spend as much time scrying as you'd like—from a few minutes to over an hour.

7. Thank your deity of choice and leave your offering: *"Goddess of the July Moon, I thank you for your presence tonight."*

8. Release the elements in reverse order by beginning facing the north and ending east, thanking each element for their assistance and bidding them farewell. Then open the circle by saying: *"I open this circle and release the energy back into the earth."*

9. Dispose of the scrying water by pouring it into the earth.

10. Extinguish the candles and incense. Leave the offering on the altar.

AUGUST MOON

Gregorian Calendar: The August moon is often called the corn, barley, red, or sturgeon moon. During this full moon, work on magic relating to abundance, health, prosperity, and renewal.

Celtic Tree Calendar: The Holly moon is celebrated until August 4 and the Hazel moon is celebrated from August 5 to September 1. The Celtic name for *hazel* is *coll*, pronounced *kol*. The Holly moon is associated with beauty, protection, luck, and dreams, and the Hazel moon is associated with manifestation, protection, knowledge, and wisdom.

PROSPERITY MANDALA ESBAT

One of the major elements of the month of August is prosperity. You can see this in the land itself; fields are full of crops as the harvest season begins. In this ritual, you'll use foraged items to create a seasonal mandala—a symbolic circular, symmetrical design—to honor the bounty of the earth and bring prosperity into your life.

Ritual Setting
Outdoors under the full moon

Tools and Supplies
Wand or athame

Elemental representations

Deity representation

Foraged decorative items for mandala—corn, barley, yellow flowers, herbs, and stones

Camera (optional)

PRIOR TO THE RITUAL

1. Shower or bathe, visualizing all old or unwanted energies leaving your being.

2. Find an outdoor space to use as an altar. Cleanse the space.

PREPARING THE ALTAR

Set up the outdoor altar space with the tools and supplies. Use a table if you'd like. Place the elemental and deity representations intuitively around the altar space.

THE RITUAL

1. Cast a circle of protection. Hold the wand or athame as an extension of your hand to gather and direct energy as you call upon the elements. Starting from the east and ending north, call upon the element of air for mental clarity, the element of fire for power, the element of water for fluidity, and the element of earth for stability.

2. Invoke the God and Goddess or deity of your choice by saying something like: *"Goddess of the Corn Moon, I invite you to my sacred circle tonight."*

3. With the foraged decorative items, begin to construct a mandala, working from the center and continuing outward. Try to make your mandala as symmetrical as possible. As you place each item, focus your thoughts and intentions on prosperity, noticing how your life reflects the Corn moon's energy. Where do you see prosperity and abundance in your own life?

4. As you complete each stage of the circular pattern, chant: *"From seed to harvest, Mother Earth, I thank you."*

5. Continue constructing the mandala. When you're finished, close your eyes and meditate for 5 to 10 minutes.

6. If you'd like, take a photograph of your mandala, as you will leave it behind.

7. Thank the Goddess: *"Goddess of the Corn Moon, I thank you for your guidance tonight."*

8. Release the elements in reverse order by beginning facing the north and ending east, thanking each element for their assistance and bidding them farewell. Then open the circle by saying: *"I open this circle and release the energy back into the earth."*

9. Return the foraged mandala to the earth as an offering.

BURN AND BANISH HEALTH ESBAT

Health and renewal are two other important themes of the August Corn moon. It's a time to take stock of your life and to focus on your spiritual and physical health. What needs to be banished from your life in order for you to feel renewed and to move forward in a positive direction?

Ritual Setting
Altar

Tools and Supplies

Wand or athame

Elemental representations

Deity representation

1 pillar or votive candle—black (for banishing)

Fire-safe plate or candle holder

Lighter or matches

Black permanent marker

4 to 6 bay leaves

Fire-safe cauldron

Offering of choice—baked goods, crafts, or foraged items

PRIOR TO THE RITUAL

1. Shower or bathe, visualizing all old or unwanted energies leaving your being.

2. Cleanse the altar.

PREPARING THE ALTAR

Place the tools and supplies on the altar. Place the elemental and deity representations intuitively around the altar space.

THE RITUAL

1. Cast a circle of protection. Hold the wand or athame as an extension of your hand to gather and direct energy as you call upon the elements. Starting from the east and ending north, call upon the element of air for mental clarity, the element of fire for power, the element of water for fluidity, and the element of earth for stability.

2. Invoke the Goddess or deity of your choice by saying something like: *"Wise Crone of the Triple Goddess, join me in my circle and lend me your wisdom and guidance."*

3. Light the black banishing candle on the fire-safe plate.

4. Reflect on your spiritual and physical health. Using the permanent marker, write on the bay leaves the things you wish to banish from your life. What's causing you burnout, fatigue, or stress?

5. Once you are finished writing, set fire to the bay leaves one at a time, using the flame of the banishing candle. Place the burning bay leaves in the fire-safe cauldron.

6. When the last bay leaf is burning, visualize everything causing you stress or difficulty being banished from your life.

7. Thank the Goddess and leave your offering: *"Wise Crone of the Triple Goddess, I thank you for your wisdom and guidance tonight."*

8. Release the elements in reverse order by beginning facing the north and ending east, thanking each element for their assistance and bidding them farewell. Then open the circle by saying: *"I open this circle and release the energy back into the earth."*

9. Extinguish the candle. Allow the bay leaves to burn out. Take any ash outside and return it to the earth as an offering.

SEPTEMBER MOON

Gregorian Calendar: The September moon is often called the harvest, wine, or singing moon. During this full moon, work on magic relating to protection, balance, emotions, well-being, and reaping what you have sown.

Celtic Tree Calendar: The Hazel moon is celebrated until September 1, and the Vine moon is celebrated from September 2 to September 29 (the Ivy moon, page 130, begins on September 30). The Celtic name for *vine* is *muin*, pronounced *mwin*. The Hazel moon is associated with manifestation, protection, knowledge, and wisdom, and the Vine moon is associated with protection, healing, and abundance.

BODY AND MIND ESBAT

September is the month of the Autumn Equinox, when the days and nights are close to equal in length. As such, the September full moon is a time of balance. Perform this ritual to balance both your body and mind.

Ritual Setting
Altar

Tools and Supplies

Wand or athame

Elemental representations

Deity representation

2 votive or pillar candles—1 black,
  1 white (to represent body and mind)

Fire-safe plates or candle holders

Lighter or matches

Bell

Offering of choice—baked goods,
  foraged items, or crafts

PRIOR TO THE RITUAL

1. Shower or bathe, visualizing all old or unwanted energies leaving your being.

2. Cleanse the altar.

PREPARING THE ALTAR

Place the tools and supplies on the altar. Place the elemental representations in a pentacle configuration. Place the deity representation at the top of the altar. Place the black and white candles in the center of the pentacle on fire-safe plates.

THE RITUAL

1. Cast a circle of protection. Hold the wand or athame as an extension of your hand to gather and direct energy as you call upon the elements. Starting from the east and ending north, call upon the element of air for mental clarity, the element of fire for power, the element of water for fluidity, and the element of earth for stability.

2. Invoke the God and Goddess or deity of your choice: *"Goddess of the Harvest Moon, I invite you to join my circle tonight."*

3. Light the white candle, ring the bell, and say: *"Candle of light and mind, burn and bring the power of peace."*

4. Light the black candle, ring the bell, and say: *"Candle of night and body, burn and bring the power of harmony."*

5. Close your eyes and visualize the energies of the candles mixing together and finding balance.

6. When you feel ready, ring the bell and say: *"Tonight, I seek balance in body and mind."*

7. Thank the Goddess and leave your offering: *"Goddess of the Harvest Moon, I thank you for your assistance tonight."*

8. Release the elements in reverse order by beginning facing the north and ending east, thanking each element for their assistance and bidding them farewell. Then open the circle by saying: *"I open this circle and release the energy back into the earth."*

9. Extinguish the candles or allow them to burn out. Leave the offering on the altar.

HARVEST ESBAT

This ritual, performed under the full Harvest moon, will help you honor the themes of gratitude, sharing, and "reaping what you've sown." With this ritual, you'll get a better look at what you've achieved through your hard work this year, using divination and the energy of the full moon to guide you in receiving and interpreting messages.

Ritual Setting
Altar

Tools and Supplies

Wand or athame

Deity representation

Elemental representations

Lighter or matches

1 cone or stick incense—cinnamon, nutmeg, sandalwood, or vanilla

Fire-safe plate or incense holder

Tarot deck, Oracle deck, or other divination system

Journal and pen

Offering of choice—baked goods, crafts, or foraged items

PRIOR TO THE RITUAL

1. Shower or bathe, visualizing all old or unwanted energies leaving your being.

2. Cleanse the altar.

PREPARING THE ALTAR

Place the tools and supplies on the altar. Place the elemental representations in a pentacle configuration. Place the deity representation at the top of the altar. Place the divination deck in the center of the pentacle.

THE RITUAL

1. Cast a circle of protection. Hold the wand or athame as an extension of your hand to gather and direct energy as you call upon the elements. Starting from the east and ending north, call upon the element of air for mental clarity, the element of fire for power, the element of water for fluidity, and the element of earth for stability.

2. Invoke the God and Goddess or deity of your choice: *"God of the Sun, Goddess of the Moon, join my circle under the Harvest full moon."*

3. Light the incense on the fire-safe plate and set your intentions.

4. Shuffle the divination deck until you feel compelled to stop.

5. Fan out the cards on the altar. Pull three cards and ask three questions: Which area of my life has improved this year? What are the benefits of my hard work? How can I reap these benefits?

6. Spend 5 to 10 minutes reflecting on the three cards, using them to help you interpret how you can reap what you've sown. Use the journal to take notes.

7. When you're finished, thank the deities for their assistance and place the offering on the altar: *"God of the Sun, Goddess of the Moon, I thank you for your presence tonight."*

8. Release the elements in reverse order by beginning facing the north and ending east, thanking each element for their assistance and bidding them farewell. Then open the circle by saying: *"I open this circle and release the energy back into the earth."*

9. Extinguish the incense or allow it to burn out. Leave the offering on the altar.

OCTOBER MOON

Gregorian Calendar: The October moon is often called the blood, shedding, falling leaf, or hunter's moon. During this full moon, work on magic relating to letting go, cleansing, karma, protection, divination, and spirits.

Celtic Tree Calendar: The Ivy moon is celebrated from September 30 to October 27 (the Reed moon, page 134, begins on October 28). The Celtic name for *ivy* is *gort,* pronounced *go-ert*. The Ivy moon is associated with healing, protection, and cooperation.

HONORING SPIRITS ESBAT

October is the month of the sabbat Samhain, during which the veil between the human world and the spiritual world is at its thinnest. A ritual honoring spirits is a great way to celebrate the Blood moon during this time. This ritual combines the energy of the full moon with offerings and deity.

Ritual Setting
Altar

Tools and Supplies

Wand or athame	Bell
Elemental representations	Cake and ale
Deity representation	

PRIOR TO THE RITUAL

1. Prepare a baked "cake" offering of your choice (e.g., moon cookies, spiced muffins, chocolate cake, or other sweets). Pour a drink of choice as your "ale."

2. Shower or bathe, visualizing all old or unwanted energies leaving your being.

3. Cleanse the altar.

PREPARING THE ALTAR

Place the tools and supplies on the altar. Place the elemental representations in a pentacle configuration. Place the deity representation at the top of the altar. Place the cake and ale in the center of the pentacle.

THE RITUAL

1. Cast a circle of protection. Hold the wand or athame as an extension of your hand to gather and direct energy as you call upon the elements. Starting from the east and ending north, call upon the element of air for mental clarity, the element of fire for power, the element of water for fluidity, and the element of earth for stability.

2. Invoke the God and Goddess or deity of your choice: *"Wise Crone of the Blood moon, I invite you to my circle tonight."*

3. Ring the bell as you say: *"Spirits of the night, join me under the Blood moon tonight; spirits through the veil, join me while the doorway is frail."*

4. Hold your offering up to the sky and say: *"Under the Blood moon, I honor you; accept my offering and brew."*

5. Taste your cake and ale.

6. Sit back and meditate for 5 to 10 minutes on your intentions.

7. Thank the Goddess: *"Wise Crone of the Blood moon, I thank you for your presence tonight."*

8. Release the elements in reverse order by beginning facing the north and ending east, thanking each element for their assistance and bidding them farewell. Then open the circle by saying: *"I open this circle and release the energy back into the earth."*

9. Cover the remaining cake and ale and leave it on the altar overnight as an offering. The next day, dispose of it by returning it to the earth.

WARDING ESBAT

The October full moon is also a good time for protection rituals. This protection ritual is performed in your kitchen and uses eggshells, which are known for their cleansing and protection properties.

Ritual Setting
Altar

Tools and Supplies

Wand or athame

Elemental representations

Deity representation

Mortar and pestle

6 to 12 eggshells

1 (8-ounce) glass jar with lid

Offering of choice—baked goods, crafts, or foraged items

PRIOR TO THE RITUAL

1. Shower or bathe, visualizing all old or unwanted energies leaving your being.

2. Cleanse the altar.

PREPARING THE ALTAR

Place the tools and supplies on the altar. Place the elemental representations in a pentacle configuration. Place the deity representation at the top of the altar.

THE RITUAL

1. Cast a circle of protection. Hold the wand or athame as an extension of your hand to gather and direct energy as you call upon the elements. Starting from the east and ending north, call upon the element of air for mental clarity, the element of fire for power, the element of water for fluidity, and the element of earth for stability.

2. Invoke the God and Goddess or deity of your choice by saying something like: *"Lord and Lady, I invite you to my circle tonight. Grant me your blessings and lend me your guidance."*

3. With your mortar and pestle, begin grinding the eggshells a few at a time to create a powder. Work clockwise to attract and "stir in" energy.

4. Once you have ground all the eggshells, pour the powder into the glass jar. Hold it up to the sky and say: *"Great Lord and Lady, imbue your strength and energy, and bless this powder with protective power."*

5. Thank the deities and leave your offering: *"Lord and Lady, I thank you for your blessings and guidance."*

6. Release the elements in reverse order by beginning facing the north and ending east, thanking each element for their assistance and bidding them farewell. Then open the circle by saying: *"I open this circle and release the energy back into the earth."*

7. Leave the offering on the altar.

8. Leave the jar open under the moonlight overnight. The next day, screw the lid shut. This jar of protective eggshell powder can be sprinkled around your home, car, or even on yourself to ward off negativity.

NOVEMBER MOON

Gregorian Calendar: The November moon is often called the mourning, frost, or beaver moon. During this full moon, work on magic relating to fresh starts, dreamwork, energy, spirit guides, meditation, and connections.

Celtic Tree Calendar: The Reed moon is celebrated from October 28 to November 23 (the Elder moon, page 138, begins on November 24). The Celtic name for *reed* is *negetal*, pronounced *nyettle*. The Reed moon is associated with healing, divination, and protection. In the Celtic calendar, November marked the new year.

FRESH START ESBAT

November is a great time to hit the reset button, mentally, spiritually, and physically. It's the month of the Celtic new year, so you can use November's full moon energy to start afresh. This ritual uses a feather or besom, a blue candle, a bowl of water, and salt to renew yourself.

Ritual Setting
Altar

Tools and Supplies

Wand or athame

Elemental representations

Deity representation

Bowl of water

Pinch salt

1 pillar or votive candle—blue

Fire-safe plate or candle holder

Lighter or matches

Feather or besom

Offering of choice—baked goods, crafts, or foraged items

PRIOR TO THE RITUAL

1. Shower or bathe, visualizing all old or unwanted energies leaving your being.

2. Cleanse the altar.

PREPARING THE ALTAR

Place the tools and supplies on the altar. Place the elemental representations in a pentacle configuration. Place the deity representation at the top of the altar. Place the water, salt, and candle (on the fire-safe plate) in the center of the pentacle.

THE RITUAL

1. Cast a circle of protection. Hold the wand or athame as an extension of your hand to gather and direct energy as you call upon the elements. Starting from the east and ending north, call upon the element of air for mental clarity, the element of fire for power, the element of water for fluidity, and the element of earth for stability.

2. Invoke the God and Goddess or deity of your choice: *"Goddess of the Mourning Moon, I invite you to my circle tonight."*

3. Light the blue candle and say: *"With this flame, I burn all that burdens me."*

4. Wave the feather upward through the heat of the flame and say: *"With this feather, I lift all that weighs on me."*

5. Sprinkle the salt into the bowl of water and say: *"With this salt, I purify all that troubles me."*

6. Hold up the bowl of water and say: *"With this water, I cleanse all that ails me."*

7. Close your eyes and focus on creating a fresh start for yourself.

8. Thank the Goddess and leave your offering: *"Goddess of the Mourning Moon, I thank you for your presence tonight."*

9. Release the elements in reverse order by beginning facing the north and ending east, thanking each element for their assistance and bidding them farewell. Then open the circle by saying: *"I open this circle and release the energy back into the earth."*

10. Extinguish the candle or allow it to burn out. Leave the offering on the altar.

ENERGY WORK ESBAT

November is a time to cultivate healing and get in touch with your inner energy. In this ritual, you'll work with your own energy so you can feel healthier and stronger than before. This is a simple ritual that involves dressing a candle and working with the energy of the full moon.

Ritual Setting
Altar

Tools and Supplies

Wand or athame

Elemental representations

Deity representation

3 crystals—clear quartz

1 taper or pillar candle—purple

1 ounce carrier oil—olive, grapeseed, or apricot kernel

1 teaspoon salt

1 teaspoon dried rosemary

Fire-safe plate or candle holder

Lighter and matches

Offering of choice—baked goods, crafts, or foraged items

PRIOR TO THE RITUAL

1. Shower or bathe, visualizing all old or unwanted energies leaving your being.

2. Cleanse the altar.

PREPARING THE ALTAR

Place the tools and supplies in the center of the altar. Place the elemental representations in a pentacle configuration. Place the deity representation at the top of the altar. Position the crystals in a triangle formation inside the pentacle.

THE RITUAL

1. Cast a circle of protection. Hold the wand or athame as an extension of your hand to gather and direct energy as you call upon the elements. Starting from the east and ending north, call upon the element of air for mental clarity, the element of fire for power, the element of water for fluidity, and the element of earth for stability.

2. Invoke the God and Goddess or deity of your choice: *"Lord and Lady, I invite you to my circle tonight."*

3. Dress the candle by pouring carrier oil down its sides. Be careful not to get oil on the wick. Sprinkle the salt and rosemary over the oiled parts of the candle.

4. Place the candle on the fire-safe plate and light it.

5. Close your eyes and focus on the candle. Visualize your energy flowing through you continuously. Practice containing and focusing on your energy for about 20 minutes.

6. Thank the deities and leave your offering: *"Lord and Lady, I thank you for your presence tonight."*

7. Release the elements in reverse order by beginning facing the north and ending east, thanking each element for their assistance and bidding them farewell. Then open the circle by saying: *"I open this circle and release the energy back into the earth."*

8. Extinguish the candle or allow it to burn out. Leave the offering on the altar.

DECEMBER MOON

Gregorian Calendar: The December moon is often called the Long Nights moon or Cold moon. During this full moon, work on magic relating to endurance, rebirth, and transformation.

Celtic Tree Calendar: The Elder moon is celebrated from November 24 to December 23 (the Birch moon, page 89, begins on December 24). The Celtic name for Elder is *ruish,* pronounced *roo-esh.* The Elder moon is associated with beginnings and endings, births and deaths, and rejuvenation.

ENDURANCE ESBAT

One of the prominent themes of the December (long nights) moon is endurance, which comes from the lengthening nights during this phase of the year. Use this ritual to improve your own endurance for times when life presents you with challenges. This ritual will help you to handle life's ups and downs so you can become stronger and more resilient.

Ritual Setting
Altar

Tools and Supplies

Wand or athame

Elemental representations

Deity representation

1 pillar candle—brown

Fire-safe plate or candle holder

Knife or boline

Uruz runestone, or other visual reference of Uruz

Lighter or matches

Offering of choice—baked goods, crafts, or foraged items

PRIOR TO THE RITUAL

1. Shower or bathe, visualizing all old or unwanted energies leaving your being.

2. Cleanse the altar.

PREPARING THE ALTAR

Place the tools and supplies on the altar. Place the elemental representations in a pentacle configuration. Place the deity representation at the top of the altar. Place the candle on the fire-safe plate in the center of the pentacle.

THE RITUAL

1. Cast a circle of protection. Hold the wand or athame as an extension of your hand to gather and direct energy as you call upon the elements. Starting from the east and ending north, call upon the element of air for mental clarity, the element of fire for power, the element of water for fluidity, and the element of earth for stability.

2. Invoke the God and Goddess or deity of your choice by saying something like: *"Deities of the Long Nights Moon, I invite you to bless this circle tonight."*

3. Using a knife or boline, carefully carve the Uruz rune symbol into the candle. Place the carved candle back on the fire-safe plate.

4. Light the candle and say: *"Endurance candle I inscribed with the Uruz rune, I burn thee to empower and strengthen mind over matter."*

5. Allow the candle to burn as you meditate for 10 to 20 minutes, focusing on building endurance.

6. Hold up your offering and thank the deities: *"Deities of the Long Nights Moon, I thank you for your assistance tonight. Please accept my offering for your guidance and wisdom."*

7. Release the elements in reverse order by beginning facing the north and ending east, thanking each element for their assistance and bidding them farewell. Then open the circle by saying: *"I open this circle and release the energy back into the earth."*

8. Extinguish the candle or allow it to burn out. Leave the offering on the altar.

REBIRTH ESBAT

In December, the nights are long, but after the Winter Solstice, the sun's strength begins to return. Because of this, the Long Nights moon is associated with rebirth and transformation. This ritual involves using a divination deck to interpret how you can seek rebirth and transformation in your own life.

Ritual Setting
Altar

Tools and Supplies
Wand or athame

Elemental representations

Deity representation

1 cone or stick incense—cinnamon, pine, cedar, fir, or juniper

Fire-safe plate or incense holder

Lighter or matches

Tarot deck, Oracle deck, or other divination system

Journal and pen

Offering of choice—baked goods, crafts, or foraged items

PRIOR TO THE RITUAL

1. Shower or bathe, visualizing all old or unwanted energies leaving your being.

2. Cleanse the altar.

PREPARING THE ALTAR

Place the tools and supplies on the altar. Place the elemental representations in a pentacle configuration. Place the deity representation at the top of the altar. Place the incense (on the fire-safe plate) and divination deck in the center of the pentacle.

THE RITUAL

1. Cast a circle of protection. Hold the wand or athame as an extension of your hand to gather and direct energy as you call upon the elements. Starting from the east and ending north, call upon the element of air for mental clarity, the element of fire for power, the element of water for fluidity, and the element of earth for stability.

2. Invoke the God and Goddess or deity of your choice by saying something like: *"God of the Sun, Goddess of the Moon, join my circle under the Long Nights Moon."*

3. Light the incense and set your intentions.

4. Shuffle the divination deck until you feel compelled to stop.

5. Fan out the cards on the altar. Pull three cards and ask three questions: What is being awakened in me after a long slumber? What will gain momentum as the days grow longer? What in myself do I fear to shed light on?

6. Spend 5 to 10 minutes reflecting on the cards, using them to interpret how you can transform yourself. Use the journal to take notes.

7. Thank the deities and leave your offering: *"God of the Sun, Goddess of the Moon, I thank you for your presence tonight."*

8. Release the elements in reverse order by beginning facing the north and ending east, thanking each element for their assistance and bidding them farewell. Then open the circle by saying: *"I open this circle and release the energy back into the earth."*

9. Extinguish the incense or allow it to burn out. Leave the offering on the altar.

THIRTEENTH MOON

A thirteenth moon, sometimes called a blue moon, occurs when a second full moon appears in one calendar month. Because the lunar cycle is slightly shorter than a calendar month, a blue moon often happens during the first few days of a month. The energy of this moon is stronger than the other moons and is often associated with intuition, wisdom, sacred femininity, and growing knowledge.

DREAM CHARM ESBAT

Because the thirteenth full moon is ethereal by nature, it provides an ideal opportunity to perform rituals that enhance your intuition, bring you wisdom, or celebrate knowledge and learning. All these elements are found in dreams. This simple ritual involves creating a charged herbal charm bag to support peaceful dreaming.

Ritual Setting
Altar

Tools and Supplies
Wand or athame

Elemental representations

Deity representation

1 votive or pillar candle—blue, for dreaming

Fire-safe plate or candle holder

Lighter or matches

Offering of choice

3 crystals—amethyst or clear quartz

FOR THE CHARM BAG
Drawstring pouch

1 ounce dried lavender

1 ounce dried peppermint

1 ounce dried chamomile

PRIOR TO THE RITUAL

1. Shower or bathe, visualizing all old or unwanted energies leaving your being.

2. Cleanse the altar.

PREPARING THE ALTAR

Place the tools and supplies on the altar. Place the elemental representations in a pentacle configuration. Place the deity representation at the top of the altar. Place the candle (on the fire-safe plate) and charm bag supplies in the center of the pentacle.

THE RITUAL

1. Cast a circle of protection. Hold the wand or athame as an extension of your hand to gather and direct energy as you call upon the elements. Starting from the east and ending north, call upon the element of air for mental clarity, the element of fire for power, the element of water for fluidity, and the element of earth for stability.

2. Invoke the God and Goddess or deity of your choice by saying: *"Mother, Maiden, and Crone, join my sacred circle."*

3. Light the candle and say: *"I invoke the power of the moon to soothe my waking mind."*

4. Put the lavender, peppermint, and chamomile in the drawstring pouch, focusing on your intentions. Once finished, chant: *"Herbal charm I charge under the blue moon, allow my sleeping mind to be at peace, so that I may now dream at ease."*

5. Tie the bag shut to complete the charm bag.

6. Thank the Goddess and leave your offering: *"Mother, Maiden, and Crone, I thank you for your assistance tonight."*

7. Release the elements in reverse order by beginning facing the north and ending east, thanking each element for their assistance and bidding them farewell. Then open the circle by saying: *"I open this circle and release the energy back into the earth."*

8. Extinguish the candle. Leave the offering on the altar.

9. Place the charm bag under the moonlight, surrounded by the crystals to further charge it with energy.

SEALING ESBAT

In this ritual, you will "seal" your good intentions using the energy of the blue moon. You'll write a note during the ritual and seal it in wax to preserve your intentions. To enhance the magic in this ritual, you'll need to use handmade tea-stained paper, prepared at least a day in advance of the ritual.

Ritual Setting

Kitchen (for preparation) and altar

Tools and Supplies

Wand or athame

Elemental representations

Deity representation

Pen and tea-stained paper

Sealing wax and stamp (or ⅔ cup beeswax, ⅓ cup resin, and a button to use as a stamp)

Lighter or matches

Offering of choice

FOR THE TEA–STAINED PAPER (PREPARED AT LEAST A DAY IN ADVANCE)

3 tea bags

2 cups water

Teapot

1 sheet paper

Rimmed baking sheet (larger than paper)

Large paintbrush (optional)

2 sheets waxed paper

Heavy object—another baking sheet or book

PRIOR TO THE RITUAL

1. Prepare the tea-stained paper.

   ➤ Brew the tea bags with the water in the teapot. While the tea brews, place the paper on the baking sheet.

   ➤ Pour the tea directly onto the paper until you achieve your desired color. If desired, for more control over the staining, use the large paintbrush to paint the tea onto the paper.

   ➤ Allow the paper to dry overnight. To prevent the paper from warping, place it between the sheets of wax paper and flatten with the heavy object.

2. Shower or bathe, visualizing all old or unwanted energies leaving your being.

3. Cleanse the altar.

PREPARING THE ALTAR

Place the tools and supplies on the altar. Place the elemental representations in a pentacle configuration. Place the deity representation at the top of the altar. Place the writing and sealing supplies in the center of the pentacle.

THE RITUAL

1. Cast a circle of protection. Hold the wand or athame as an extension of your hand to gather and direct energy as you call upon the elements. Starting from the east and ending north, call upon the element of air for mental clarity, the element of fire for power, the element of water for fluidity, and the element of earth for stability.

2. Invoke your deity of choice by saying something like: *"Goddess of the Thirteenth Moon, join me in my circle and lend me your insight."*

3. Write a letter on the tea-stained paper, discussing the things you want to manifest in your life.

4. Once you have finished writing, fold the paper from the top and bottom so that one end overlaps the other, allowing you to place a wax seal.

5. Hold a flame to the sealing wax and let it drip onto the overlapped portion of the paper. Focus on your intentions to attract and manifest.

6. Once the wax has started to dry, press the stamp into the wax. Place the letter on the altar.

CONTINUED

7. When you are ready, thank the Goddess and leave your offering: *"Goddess of the Thirteenth Moon, I thank you for your insight tonight."*

8. Release the elements in reverse order by beginning facing the north and ending east, thanking each element for their assistance and bidding them farewell. Then open the circle by saying: *"I open this circle and release the energy back into the earth."*

9. Keep the letter on the altar until the things you wrote have manifested. Leave the offering on the altar.

CHAPTER 7
WICCAN RITES

Both Wiccan rituals and rites are forms of ceremony, but Wiccan rites focus specifically on important transitional periods in a person's life, such as birth, marriage, and death. Rites are often more formal than rituals, though not always. This chapter will detail common Wiccan rites and basic instructions for how to perform them, but each rite can be modified to suit your particular practice.

DEDICATION

Dedication is the practice of devoting time or effort to a particular purpose. In Wicca, this translates to dedicating yourself under oath to the religion and its practices. Many Wiccans choose to perform a formal self-dedication ritual when they begin practicing, though others simply start identifying as Wiccan. If you feel inclined to ceremonially validate your entrance into Wicca, a dedication ritual may well suit you.

Remember that the only person that makes you "officially" Wiccan is you, so as you prepare to perform a dedication, you should be spiritually ready to make a commitment to the craft on your own terms. If you want to follow a specific, established tradition rather than your own eclectic practice, you can often find dedication or initiation rites in books or from members of a coven.

DEDICATION RITE

This is a formal ceremony in which one dedicates oneself to the practice of Wicca and to deity. Some Wiccans opt to perform their dedication rite on the night of a new moon, whereas others choose a day when they feel ready.

Rite Setting
Altar or outdoors

Tools and Supplies

Wand or athame

5 taper or votive candles—in elemental colors (alternatively, use crystals)

Fire-safe plates or candle holders and incense holder

Lighter or matches

Deity representation—statues, candles, or images of the God and Goddess

1 cone or stick incense—peppermint, frankincense, pine, myrrh, bayberry, or cinnamon

Blessing oil

Offering of choice—bread, baked goods, crafted items, or foraged flowers and herbs

FOR THE BLESSING OIL

1 ounce carrier oil (e.g., jojoba or olive)

6 drops frankincense essential oil

Small glass bottle with lid

PRIOR TO THE RITE

1. Shower or bathe, visualizing all old or unwanted energies leaving your being. If you wish, you can use soaps or bath bombs to enhance purification for this rite.

2. Wear special clothing or a ritual robe to further distinguish and elevate this rite from other rituals.

3. Cleanse the altar.

4. Blend together the blessing oil by combining the carrier oil and essential oil in the glass bottle.

PREPARING THE ALTAR

Set up the altar with the tools and supplies. Place the elemental candles on fire-safe plates in a pentacle configuration or facing their respective cardinal directions. Light the candles. Place the deity representation at the top of the altar.

THE RITE

1. Cast a circle of protection. Hold the wand or athame as an extension of your hand to gather and direct energy as you call upon the elements. Starting from the east and ending north, call upon the element of air for mental clarity, the element of fire for power, the element of water for fluidity, and the element of earth for stability.

2. Invoke your chosen deity by saying: *"Lord and Lady, I invite you to join this circle tonight. Lend me your guidance and grant me your blessings."*

3. Light the incense on a fire-safe plate and meditate for 10 to 20 minutes, thinking about what it means to dedicate yourself to Wicca.

CONTINUED

4. When you feel ready, dip your fingers in the blessing oil. Anoint your forehead and say your commitment and promise to the elements and deity of your choice: *"I pledge my dedication to the elements, the divine, and this path. Guide me on this journey and walk beside me. As I will it, so mote it be."*

5. Thank your deity of choice for their presence tonight: *"Lord and Lady, I thank you for your presence and assistance tonight. Accept the offering I created for you and go if you desire or stay if you'd like."*

6. Extinguish and release the elements in reverse order by beginning facing the north and ending east, thanking each element for their assistance and bidding them farewell. Then open the circle by saying: *"I open this circle and release the energy back into the earth."*

7. Extinguish the candles and incense or allow them to burn out.

8. Cover the offering overnight. The next day, dispose of any cooked or foraged offering items by burning them or returning them to the earth. Take any offerings with nonorganic materials to a landfill or recycle them appropriately.

APPRECIATION

A Wiccan appreciation rite is a great way to show your gratitude and thanks for nature, divinity, and spirits. This is a formal ceremony in which you give thanks and voice your appreciation for all that Wicca stands for. Some Wiccans use this rite to honor deities of their chosen pantheon or pantheons.

APPRECIATION CEREMONY

This ceremony can be used to celebrate nature, deity, the elements, or gratitude. You can perform this rite any time of the year, but an excellent time is during one of the harvest sabbats because the theme of gratitude is in the air.

Rite Setting
Altar or outdoors

Tools and Supplies

Wand or athame

Elemental representations—bowl of salt, to represent earth; bowl of water, to represent water; feather, to represent air; candle or incense, to represent fire; clear quartz or other white crystal, to represent spirit

Deity representation—statues, candles, or symbols of the God and Goddess or deity of your choice

Fire-safe plates or candle holder or incense holder

Lighter or matches

Cauldron or bowl

Offering of choice—bread, baked goods, crafted items, or foraged flowers and herbs

PRIOR TO THE RITE

1. Shower or bathe, visualizing all old or unwanted energies leaving your being.

2. Wear a special outfit or a ritual robe to distinguish and elevate this rite from other rituals.

3. Cleanse the altar.

CONTINUED

PREPARING THE ALTAR

Place the tools and supplies on the altar. Place the elemental objects in a pentacle configuration or facing their respective cardinal directions (place the spirit representation in the center). Place the deity representation at the top of the altar.

THE RITE

1. Cast a circle of protection. Hold the wand or athame as an extension of your hand to gather and direct energy as you call upon the elements. Starting from the east and ending north, call upon the element of air for mental clarity, the element of fire for power, the element of water for fluidity, and the element of earth for stability.

2. Invoke your deity of choice by saying something like: *"Deity, I welcome you to my circle of appreciation tonight so that I can share with you my gratitude."*

3. Sprinkle the salt into the cauldron and say: *"Thank you, element of earth, for the strength and stability you give."*

4. Sprinkle the water into the cauldron and say: *"Thank you, element of water, for the fluidity and emotions you share."*

5. Drop the feather into the cauldron saying: *"Thank you, element of air, for the clarity and guidance you give."*

6. Light the candle. Hold the candle above the cauldron and tilt it until wax begins to pour into the cauldron, and say: *"Thank you, element of fire, for the power and spark you share."*

7. Place the crystal in the cauldron and say: *"Thank you, element of spirit, for being within and all around me."*

8. Close your eyes and say: *"Diety, I thank you for the wisdom you share and the blessings you give."*

9. Meditate for 10 to 20 minutes, remembering all the things you're thankful for.

10. Hold your offering up to the sky and say: *"Deity, go if you must or stay if you like, but accept my offering of gratitude for all that you do."*

11. Release the elements in reverse order. Begin facing the north and ending east, thanking each element for their assistance and bidding them farewell.

12. Turn back to the north to release spirit and open the circle: *"Spirit, I bid you farewell. I open this circle and release the energy back into the earth."*

13. Extinguish the candle. Cover the offering and leave it on the altar overnight. Dispose of any cooked or foraged items by returning them to the earth or burning them. Take any offerings with inorganic materials to a landfill or recycle them appropriately.

HANDFASTING AND HANDPARTING

A handfasting is a Wiccan wedding ceremony that symbolically ties two people together, whereas a handparting (or Parting of Ways) is a Wiccan divorce, or a symbolic severing of ties. A handfasting is not the same as a legal wedding; it can be purely ceremonial, or it can be incorporated into the process of obtaining a legal marriage certificate. Because of their formal nature, handfastings and handpartings are usually performed by High Priests or Priestesses, officiants, or clergypersons.

HANDFASTING

Handfasting originates from a Celtic tradition in which two partners cross arms and join hands, creating a symbol of infinity that is then bound with ribbon. This tradition is where the modern phrase "tying the knot" comes from. An important note: This ceremony is a basic rite and can be altered to meet your preferences or needs. It is usually performed by a leader or officiant.

Rite Setting
Altar or outdoors

Tools and Supplies

Ceremonial décor

Wand or athame

Elemental representations (optional)

Deity representation—candles or statues (optional)

1 taper or votive candle—white, to represent unity

Fire-safe plate or candle holder

Lighter or matches

Ribbon or cord—at least a few feet, to allow wrapping

Cake and ale (optional)

PRIOR TO THE RITE

1. Choose an area, indoors or outdoors, to use as an altar for the ceremony.

2. The couple should take a purification bath or shower and prepare themselves for the ceremony.

3. Cleanse the ceremony area.

PREPARING THE ALTAR

Place the decorations around the ceremony area. Place the tools and supplies on the altar. If using, place the deity representation at the top of the altar, and place the elemental representations facing their respective cardinal directions.

THE RITE

1. The officiant or leader of the ceremony uses a wand or athame to cast a circle of protection, silently or out loud, and visualizes energy creating a wall around the area.

2. The officiant starts with the element of air for mental clarity, the element of fire for power, the element of water for fluidity, and the element of earth for stability.

3. The officiant then invokes the deity: *"Lord and Lady, we invite you to join this ceremony. Grant us your blessings and share your wisdom."*

4. The officiant visualizes loving, positive energy flowing around the area. They then discuss the ritual and the meaning of infinite love and share information about the couple.

5. Next, they light the unity candle on the fire-safe plate and say: *"Divine light, shine upon this union and bless this ceremony."*

6. The officiant then invites the couple to join hands, symbolizing their willing choice to enter into the marriage: *"I invite you two to willingly cross your hands over each other and take one another's hands."*

7. The couple then read their vows to one another. As the vows are read, the officiant wraps the ribbon around the couple's hands and then ties it, completing the bonding part of the ceremony. The officiant says: *"This ribbon symbolizes life, love, and the eternal bond you share. With your vows and this ribbon, you are now bound together as one."*

CONTINUED

8. The couple can exchange rings and kiss.

9. The officiant can then unwrap the ribbon from the couple's hands, leaving the knot intact.

10. The officiant thanks the deity for their presence: *"Lord and Lady, we thank you for your guidance. Go if you desire or stay if you'd like."*

11. The officiant then releases the elements in reverse order, beginning facing the north and ending east, thanking each element for their assistance and bidding them farewell. Then they open the circle by saying: *"The circle is opened, and energy is released back into the earth."*

12. Allow the unity candle to burn out. Keep the handfasting ribbon for the duration of the relationship.

13. If desired, have a reception with cake and ale.

HANDPARTING

The "parting of ways" ceremony is used to mark the end of a relationship or commitment. If a handfasting (page 156) was done previously, a parting of ways ceremony, or handparting, is a good way to sever the bond. This ritual is simple and straightforward, and it uses the same handfasting ribbon from the original handfasting ceremony. It is usually performed by a leader or officiant.

Rite Setting
Altar or outdoors

Tools and Supplies:
Wand or athame

Elemental representations (optional)

Deity representation (optional)

Ribbon or cord from original handfasting ceremony

Boline or scissors

PRIOR TO THE RITE
1. Choose an area, indoors or outdoors, to use as an altar for the ceremony.

2. The participants should take a purification bath or shower and prepare themselves for the ceremony.

3. Cleanse the ceremony area.

PREPARING THE ALTAR
Place the decorations around the ceremony area. Place the tools and supplies on the altar. Place the elemental representations facing their respective cardinal directions, and place the deity representation (if using) at the top of the altar.

THE RITE
1. The officiant or leader of the ceremony uses a wand or athame to cast a circle of protection, silently or out loud, and visualizes energy creating a wall around the area.

CONTINUED

2. The officiant calls upon the element of air for mental clarity, the element of fire for power, the element of water for fluidity, and the element of earth for stability.

3. The officiant then invokes the deity of your choice by saying: *"Lord and Lady, we invite you to bear witness and lend us your guidance."*

4. The officiant then asks the couple: *"Why have you come here?"*

5. The couple must each speak sincerely, explaining the circumstances that make them ready to end the commitment.

6. The officiant then holds the handfasting ribbon and says: *"This ribbon symbolizes life, love, and the eternal bond you share. With this boline, we sever the bond and free you to go your separate ways."*

7. The officiant cuts the knot in the ribbon, symbolically severing the commitment.

8. The officiant thanks the deity for their presence: *"Lord and Lady, we thank you for your guidance. Go if you desire or stay if you'd like."*

9. Next, the officiant releases the elements in reverse order, beginning facing north and ending east, thanking each element for their assistance and bidding them farewell. Then they open the circle by saying: *"The circle is opened, and energy is released back into the earth."*

10. The handparting ceremony is complete, and both parties can go their separate ways.

WICCANING

A Wiccaning is a ceremony in which an infant or child is welcomed into the Wiccan community. It's often called a baby blessing, baby naming ceremony, or a *saining*, a Scottish word that means "to bless, consecrate, or protect." A Wiccaning is similar to a baptism or christening, common in Christian faith, although a Wiccaning does not commit the child to any religion. The choice to become Wiccan is entirely up to the individual, so if a child has a Wiccaning, they can still choose whether to practice Wicca later in life. Wiccanings are sometimes performed by High Priests or Priestesses, and sometimes by the child's parents.

WICCANING

Rite Setting
Altar or outdoors

Tools and Supplies

Wand or athame

Elemental representations

Deity representation

1 pillar candle—white

Fire-safe plate or candle holder

Lighter or matches

Bowl of full moon charged water (see page 88)

Offering of choice—bread, baked goods, crafted items, or foraged flowers and herbs

Cake and ale (optional)

PRIOR TO THE RITE

1. Choose an area, indoors or outdoors, to use as an altar for the ceremony.

2. All participants should take a purification bath or shower and prepare themselves for the ceremony. The parents and child should wear ritual robes or other special occasion clothing for the ceremony.

3. Cleanse the ceremony area.

CONTINUED

PREPARING THE ALTAR

Place the tools and supplies on the altar. Place the elemental representations facing their respective cardinal directions. Place the deity representation at the top of the altar.

THE RITE

1. The parents should carry their child to the altar, and the rest of the coven and/or guests should form a circle around them.

2. A High Priest or Priestess (or the parents, if they are taking on the role of High Priest and Priestess) uses a wand or athame to cast a circle of protection silently or out loud and visualizes energy creating a wall around the area.

3. The leader of the ceremony, silently or out loud, calls upon the element of air for mental clarity, the element of fire for power, the element of water for fluidity, and the element of earth for stability.

4. They then invoke the chosen deity by saying something like: *"Deity, we invite you to join this circle tonight. Lend us your guidance and grant us your blessings."*

5. The parents then light the candle on the fire-safe plate and say: *"We stand at the altar to present our child, asking for the guidance and blessing of the Lord and Lady until the day he/she chooses their own path."*

6. The leader of the ceremony then anoints the child's forehead with full moon charged water. The leader then says: *"May you be blessed, loved, and cherished. May you carry joy and be in good health."*

7. Anyone else who wishes to give their blessings should do so.

8. The leader thanks the deity for their presence: *"Deity, we thank you for your presence and assistance tonight. Accept our offering and go if you desire or stay if you'd like."*

9. The leader releases the elements in reverse order, beginning facing the north and ending east, thanking each element for their assistance and bidding them farewell. Then they open the circle by saying: *"The circle is opened, and energy is released back into the earth."*

10. Extinguish the candle or allow it to burn out. Leave the offering on the altar until the ceremony is over.

11. If desired, have a celebratory reception with cake and ale.

FUNERAL CEREMONY

A funeral ceremony, often called a Summerland service, rite, or ritual, will help you and your loved ones find peace in the wake of a death. This rite also provides an opportunity to celebrate your loved one's life in a group setting, facilitating the great healing found in shared mourning and shared memories.

FUNERAL CEREMONY

This ceremony can be done to honor deceased loved ones at any time of year. A Wiccan funeral ceremony resembles a traditional funeral by often including a eulogy, poetry readings, and prayers to a deity. Funeral ceremonies are sometimes led by High Priests or Priestesses, officiants, or clergypersons.

Rite Setting
Altar or outdoors

Tools and Supplies
Altar decorations—flowers, photos, notes, heirlooms, and mementos

Wand or athame

Elemental representations

Deity representation

1 pillar candle—white or black (to represent the departed)

Fire-safe plate or candle holder

Lighter or matches

Cake and ale (optional)

PRIOR TO THE RITE
1. Choose an area, indoors or outdoors, to use as an altar for the ceremony.

2. All participants should take a purification bath or shower and prepare themselves for the ceremony. It's common to wear robes or other special-occasion clothing.

3. Cleanse the ceremony area.

PREPARING THE ALTAR

Decorate the designated altar space with photographs, notes, heirlooms, mementos, and flowers for your loved one who has passed. Guests are welcome to bring flowers or photographs to adorn the altar table. Place the tools and supplies on the altar. Place the elemental and deity representations intuitively around the altar space and surrounding ceremonial area. Place the candle on the fire-safe plate in the center of the altar space, among the decorations.

THE RITE

1. The leader of the ceremony uses a wand or athame to cast a circle of protection silently or out loud and visualizes energy creating a wall around the area.

2. The leader, silently or out loud, calls upon the element of air for mental clarity, the element of fire for power, the element of water for fluidity, and the element of earth for stability.

3. The leader invokes the chosen deity by saying something like: *"Deity, we invite you to join this circle tonight. Lend us your guidance and grant us your blessings."*

4. The leader of the ceremony lights the candle representing the departed. They then introduce the ceremony by saying something like: *"Merry Meet. We gather together today to honor the memory of (name), who has departed our beloved Earth."*

5. The leader reads a poem and gives blessings and a eulogy.

6. The leader invites friends and family to give eulogies or blessings: *"If anyone would like to share their thoughts, prayers, or memories, now would be the time to do so."*

7. Allow enough time for all mourners to say their goodbyes.

CONTINUED

8. At the end of the ceremony, the leader thanks the deity for their presence: *"Deity, we thank you for your presence and blessings. We welcome you to go if you desire or stay if you'd like."*

9. The leader releases the elements in reverse order, beginning facing the north and ending east, thanking each element for their assistance and bidding them farewell. Then the leader opens the circle by saying: *"The circle is opened and energy is released back into the earth. Merry meet, merry part, and merry meet again."*

10. Allow the candle to burn out. Leave the decorations in the altar space until the ceremony is over.

11. If desired, have a reception with cake and ale.

GLOSSARY

ALTAR a designated flat surface to perform rituals or other magical workings

ASPERGING sprinkling water around an altar or space for purification purposes

ATHAME a consecrated, ceremonial ritual blade used to direct energy, not to cut; usually double-edged and black-handled and can be used interchangeably with a wand during casting and opening a circle of protection

BANISH to end or get rid of negative energy or unwanted spirits

BELL often used as a ritual tool to raise energy

BESOM a broom used to sweep energy and can cleanse or purify a space

BIND to magically restrain

BLUE MOON the second of two full moons that occur in one calendar month

BOLINE a knife, often with a curved blade and white handle, used in magic and ritual for purposes such as cutting herbs, string, or knots

BOOK OF SHADOWS a witch's book of spells, rituals, and magical lore

CALLING invoking elemental or divine energy

CALLING THE QUARTERS verbal or symbolic acknowledgment of the elements in a ritual environment

CAULDRON a vessel used to hold ingredients for ritual workings; fire-safe cauldrons should be used for rituals involving fire

CHALICE a ritual cup or goblet used to hold ritual drinks, such as the "ale" in cake and ale ceremonies

CHANTS repeating phrases or words in spells or ritual to raise energy

CHARGE to infuse an object with energy

CHARMS an item created for a specific magical use; can be sachet bags, spell jars, amulets, talismans, or knots

CIRCLE a sacred, protected space created with energy to perform rituals

CLEANSING removing negative energy from an object or space

COVEN a group of Wiccans that work together to learn, grow, and perform rituals and ceremonies

CRAFT the practice of witchcraft

CRONE one of the three aspects of the Goddess, represented by the old woman and the darkest part of the year

CROSS-QUARTER DAYS the sabbats that occur between the solstices and equinoxes—Imbolc, Beltane, Lughnasadh, and Samhain

DEDICATION a ritual or rite in which an individual chooses to make an oath to accept their path as Wiccan or witch; not to be confused with initiation

DIVINATION the act of connecting to one's inner self and the universe to seek answers; divination can be done through scrying, dowsing, using Tarot or Oracle decks, casting runestones, and reading Ogham staves

DRAWING DOWN THE MOON a ritual performed during the full moon

DRAWING DOWN THE SUN a ritual performed during Litha or the Summer Solstice

DUMB SUPPER a silent or "dumb" dinner feast to honor the dead

ELEMENTS the physical elements of earth, air, fire, water that make up the building blocks of the universe. The fifth element, spirit, exists in all the physical elements and in the divine.

ESBAT a circle or ritual to honor the full moon, often used to celebrate the Goddess aspect of divinity

FULL MOON CHARGED WATER water that has been allowed to sit overnight to charge under the light of the full moon

GARDNERIAN WICCA a tradition of witchcraft created from the teachings of Gerald Gardner

GOD the masculine aspect of deity

GODDESS the feminine aspect of deity

GRIMOIRE a magical workbook or journal containing ritual information, notes, and ritual properties

GROUNDING to disperse excess energy generated during rituals by sending it into the earth

HANDFASTING a Pagan wedding ceremony

HERBALISM the art of using herbs, both magically and medicinally

HIGH PRIEST/HIGH PRIESTESS a coven leader who has reached a certain high level of initiation in their coven

HORNED GOD one of the most prevalent God-images in Paganism, one not associated with the Christian devil or Satanism

INCANTATION words spoken during rituals or spells

INCENSE herbs, oils, or other aromatic items that can be burned to scent, cleanse, or purify space during acts of ritual

INITIATION a process by which an individual is accepted or admitted to a coven; not to be confused with dedication

INVOCATION to bring or call something, such as a deity, to assist you

KABBALAH is a form of ancient Jewish mysticism. The name comes from the Hebrew word meaning "to receive." According to Judaism, Kabbalah predates Jewish Creation. Sometimes stylized with a *Q* as Qabalah. The spelling Qabalah is more often used by occultists.

KARMA the belief that a person's actions can be counted toward or against them on their spiritual path across several lifetimes

LIBATION ritually giving a portion of food or drink to a deity or spirit; often called an offering or cake and ale offering

MAGIC the projection of natural energy or power to bring about change

MAIDEN one of the three aspects of the Goddess, represented by a young woman or girl who has not yet awakened

MEDITATION a quiet time, reflection, or contemplation spent turning inward toward the self or divinity

MOTHER one of three aspects of the Goddess representing motherhood, midlife, and fertility

NEW AGE the mixing of newer spiritual practices with traditional religion

OCCULT a term meaning "hidden" that applies broadly to a wide range of metaphysical topics often misunderstood by the general population

OGHAM is the ancient alphabet of the Celtic people. Ogham is often carved into wood pieces to create Ogham staves, similar to runestones and "cast" to gain insights and information.

OLD RELIGION a name for Paganism, as it predates Christianity; sometimes also called the Old Ways

ORACLE a divination deck of varying size that uses symbolism to connect the user with their subconscious and the universe

PAGAN/NEOPAGAN a general term for followers of Wicca and any other magical, shamanistic, or polytheistic Earth-based religion

PANTHEON a collection or group of Gods and Goddesses in a particular religious structure; examples are Celtic, Roman, Greek, African, or Scandinavian

PENTACLE a circle with a five-pointed upright star, often used or worn as a symbol of a witch's beliefs; it can also be used to represent the element of earth in ritual

QABALAH is an esoteric tradition that involves the occult and mysticism (sometimes called Hermetic Qabalah). Qabalah combines elements of Kabbalah, Egyptology, divination, Tarot, and astrology. Often thought of as a precursor to Neopagan, Wiccan, and New Age movements.

QUARTERS the north, south, east, and west parts of a circle or ritual area. The quarters are the Guardians of the physical elements. The terms quarters, elements, and cardinal directions are used interchangeably when casting a circle.

REDE is the Basic tenet of Wicca, summarized as *"An it harm none, do what ye will."*

RITUAL a ceremony or rite to honor divinity and raise and use energy for an intended purpose or celebration

RITUAL TOOLS objects used in ritual and placed on an altar; they often include deity and elemental representations

RUNES a set of symbols or letters used for divination; examples are Scandinavian, Norse, and Germanic

SABBAT a sun celebration including a solstice, equinox, or cross-quarter day

SCRYING a method of divination involving gazing at or into an object or surface to receive images or messages

SKYCLAD celebrating or performing rituals in the nude

SMUDGE STICK a bundle of dried herbs, often white sage, the smoke of which is used to banish unwanted energy

SOLITARY a Pagan who often practices alone rather than as part of a coven

SPELL a magical manipulation of energy to create an intended outcome; often implements charms, sachets, herbalism, and incantations or chants

SUMMERLAND the Pagan afterlife

TAROT a 78-card divination deck that uses symbolism to connect the user with their own subconscious and the universe

THREEFOLD LAW a karmic principle that states that when a person releases energy out into the world, it will be returned to them three times

TRADITION a given branch of Paganism, often in the form of a coven or group, that follows a specific path

TRIPLE GODDESS: a Goddess in all her three aspects: Maiden, Mother, and Crone

VISUALIZATION the process of forming mental images to raise and harness energy for an intended purpose

WAND a ritual tool used to direct energy; can be used interchangeably with an athame

WHEEL OF THE YEAR a full cycle of the seasonal year that includes the eight Wiccan sabbats

WICCA a modern Pagan religion with spiritual roots; emerged in the 1950s

WICCANING a ceremony to bless a baby or child and welcome them to the Wiccan religion

WITCH a practitioner of magic, often one that uses crystals, colors, herbs, energy, and ritual

WITCHCRAFT the craft of a witch, often implementing crystals, colors, herbs, energy, and incantations

RESOURCES

A Book of Pagan Prayer by Ceisiwr Serith

This is a beautiful collection of nearly 500 prayers written to fulfill the needs of contemporary Pagans from a variety of traditions. This resource will assist in inspiring you to create invocations, incantations, songs, and chants for your practice.

The Complete Book of Incense, Oils & Brews by Scott Cunningham

This is one of my personal favorites. After you learn the basics about how herbs, spices, and plants can be used in your practice, this book will take your craft a step further and assist you in creating custom incense blends, magical oils, potions, and other useful brews.

Cunningham's Encyclopedia of Crystal, Gem & Metal Magic by Scott Cunningham

Working with the natural elements of the earth is a major part of any Wiccan's practice. This book of over 100 stones and metals will help you figure out which crystal, gem, or metal will work best in your spell.

Cunningham's Encyclopedia of Magical Herbs by Scott Cunningham

This is a must for any beginner of Wicca. It contains properties, history, and uses for over 400 herbs. Use this encyclopedia whenever you need to incorporate herbs in your spells.

The Spell Book for New Witches: Essential Spells to Change Your Life by Ambrosia Hawthorn

This spell book for beginners gives new spell-casters all the introductory information they need to get started, as well as 100 easy spells to create change in their lives. This is a great resource for any Pagan who wants to learn more about energy, magic, and manifesting change.

Wicca Magical Deities: A Guide to the Wiccan God and Goddess, and Choosing a Deity to Work Magic With by Lisa Chamberlin

Working with deities is a major part of the Wiccan religion. Chamberlin's guide for choosing deities to work with will benefit any Wiccan's practice. She gives great advice to support you as you learn to forge your own spiritual connection with the divine.

Witchology Magazine

This monthly magazine for modern Paganism and magic is a valuable resource to learn from a team of seasoned writers who share their own paths with their readers.

INDEX

ACKNOWLEDGMENTS

My thanks go to the amazing support team who helped me write this book: my wonderful partner, Leon, who encouraged me during the entire writing process; my adorable familiar Nala, who sat with me every day while I wrote this book; my amazing sister Sylvia, who always pushes me to be the best that I can; and the Witchology team for continuing to create amazing work for the magazine during my absence. Lastly, thanks to Natasha Yglesias, my editor, for her wonderful skill in making the words in this book come alive.

ABOUT THE AUTHOR

AMBROSIA HAWTHORN is a traveling eclectic Pagan, astrologer, and card slinger with indigenous roots in Yup'ik shamanism and Puerto Rican folk magic. She is the owner of Wild Goddess Magick, a witchcraft blog, and the editor of *Witchology Magazine*. She found her practice at the age of 13 and has been studying the craft and her lineage ever since. Ambrosia's goal is to provide material for every kind of Pagan, and she uses the Wheel of the Year to create and share new content about all types of magic.

CPSIA information can be obtained
at www.ICGtesting.com
Printed in the USA
JSHW061417150922
30453JS00001B/2